SMILE ON YOUR BROTHER

A FAMILY STILL HEARS THE ECHOES OF VIETNAM

SMILE ON YOUR BROTHER

A FAMILY STILL HEARS THE ECHOES OF VIETNAM

AUSTIN J. NICHOLL

Book Design: Megan Honda
Editor: Susan Nicholl

Copyright C 2013 by Austin J. Nicholl
Wintergreen Street Press
All Rights Reserved

ISBN: 0-9896474-0-4
ISBN-13: 978-0-9896474-0-3
Library of Congress Control Number: 2013949662
Wintergreen Street Press, Chicago, IL

"I loved my brother, as only the poor and lonely can love those with whom they have toiled and struggled up the rugged hill of life's success - but he died bravely in the discharge of his duty."

– Simon Cameron,
Secretary of War, 1861-1862

"Brother, brother, brother, there's far too many of you dying."

– Marvin Gaye,
singer, songwriter, and musician

For two brothers named Timmy.

CONTENTS

CHAPTER ONE - FOUNDATION 1

CHAPTER TWO - REVELATION 29

CHAPTER THREE - RESOLUTION 51

CHAPTER FOUR - DEVOTION 75

CHAPTER FIVE - APPREHENSION................... 93

CHAPTER SIX - DISSOLUTION 115

CHAPTER SEVEN - DISTINCTION.................. 135

CHAPTER EIGHT - DEVASTATION................. 151

CHAPTER NINE - CONCESSION.................... 165

CHAPTER TEN - ISOLATION 181

CHAPTER ELEVEN - CONTINUATION 217

CHAPTER TWELVE - CONNECTION 253

CHAPTER THIRTEEN - COMMEMORATION ... 267

AFTERWORD 279

EPILOGUE 303

FOREWORD

My dad was a wonderful storyteller. Often times he told the same stories over and over again with a bit of a twist; some even in song. Dad had a great tenor voice and often without any warning or notice, he would just burst into song. Each evening, he related the events of his work day at dinner by changing his voice when a different character was speaking. I would ask him to repeat favorite stories that I enjoyed hearing and dad would accommodate my request. I loved to listen to him.

My brothers, Timmy and Jack, inherited dad's skill. My brothers were very funny. It was great to be with them when they got going. We laughed a lot when we were all together. We called Timmy's stories "Timmy Tales." Like dad, he sang very well and always very loud.

All of those stories stopped when Timmy was killed in Vietnam on May 9, 1968. Dad and Jack got quiet as all of us did. The stories ended for us, as did the songs.

After Jack died in 2007, I realized that it was time for me to start telling the hardest story that I knew. I wanted to tell my family about how it was for all of us back in 1968. I used the mementos that were saved by my mom and dad to make a family book about Timmy with the support of my husband and the assistance of my son, Dennis. For the first time in well over forty years, I shared painful memories from that difficult event. I made sure that I included as much detail as possible. My four sons, my three nieces and two nephews had

FOREWORD

many unanswered questions about their uncle and about his death in Vietnam.

When Austin Nicholl approached Maureen and me about writing a book about Timmy, I realized that it was important for our family to get Timmy's story told. I am very grateful to Austin for his skillful questioning that helped me to remember events and emotions that I avoided thinking about for many years. He was also consistently sensitive to my feelings during the remembering process. He made the storytelling happen for me.

Austin was wonderful at tapping into the stories of our additional family members and Timmy's friends. More importantly, Austin was able to connect with the Marines of Mike 3/5, Timmy's unit in Vietnam. We had included the website of Mike 3/5 in our family book so we knew the terrible story of those Marines. Austin was successful in meeting with many of those Marines who served with Timmy and was able to connect in a special way with them. I'm sure their story was painful for them to share also but as with me, it was time to tell that story as well.

It is now forty-five years since Timmy was killed in Vietnam. It took a very long time for me to tell his story. Many who cared about my brother have shared their memories, a very painful task. Not only did our family treasure and honor Timmy's memory but many significant others have also. Sharing his story binds us all in love for my brother.

I smile thinking about him and treasure the moments that I shared with him. I believe that telling his story has brought him back to me. You see, today I can hear him laughing. I wasn't able to hear his laugh for such a long time. I hear him now and I smile on my brother.

– Ellen Fitzmaurice Shea
November, 2013

FOREWORD

It is very funny how your mind works. Memories can trigger emotions that you thought were long suppressed, bringing them back like it was yesterday. You find yourself remembering little details -- the smile you miss seeing, the laugh that you want to hear again, and the arms that you want to enfold you in a loving embrace. Remembering and talking about the events in this book have brought back those details and I can see Timmy, mom, dad, grandma, and grandpa clearly again. If I close my eyes I can hear them. I still miss them and will do so for the rest of my life.

This book was a labor of love. It is the story of a regular family on the northwest side of Chicago in 1968. Maybe we weren't "regular" as compared to some, but our house on Kewanee Avenue was what we knew and it was most certainly our home. We were secure in the fact that our parents loved us very much and that there was nothing they wouldn't do to keep us safe and happy. Even with the hard times, there was no doubt that we were the focus. We made their lives worthwhile. Our grandparents lived downstairs and the eight of us were a family. We loved, laughed, cried, and lived together as one unit. Life was hard at times, but we didn't let that stop us. We had each other.

I was ten years old in May, 1968. It was the end of fifth grade -- a big time for a Catholic girl. I was confirmed in April and had my first pair of nylons (which was a big deal in 1968). I was looking forward to summer -- that carefree time that all children crave. I couldn't wait for all the fun

FOREWORD

that was waiting for me in just a few more weeks. But that didn't happen. My world came crashing down one morning with a knock at the door that brought the devastating news to us about Timmy. My childhood ended that day. Gone was the girl that looked forward to a carefree summer and in her place was the girl who lost her precious and beloved big brother. My family was changed forever. I was changed forever.

When Austin first approached my sister, Ellen, and I about writing this book, my first reaction was "no way". This was our story and no one needs to know about our life. But, after thinking it over, I realized that this is a story that needs to be told. It is right for my children, and their children, to learn about a piece of their family history. In addition, it is time that the story of the Vietnam War and its aftermath was told. Our family was not alone -- there are over 58,000 families that lost their loved ones and more importantly, this story needs to be told for the ones who came home. The way that these returning soldiers and their families were treated was shameful. It is a national disgrace and must never be repeated. It is time for their stories to be heard. It is time for them to heal. It is time for all of us to heal.

To my husband, Dave, and our beautiful children, Laurel, Kristen, Kathleen, and Michael, and to my son-in-law, Aaron, and my unborn grandchildren, this story is part of who I am. It is the story how the events of May, 1968 made me who I am today.

– Maureen Fitzmaurice Schiesser
November, 2013

PREFACE

Sometimes I ask myself why I bothered them. Why did I make them go back and revisit some of the most trying and difficult times of their lives? Lance Corporal Timothy George Fitzmaurice of the United States Marine Corps was killed in Vietnam over 45 years ago. Why would I believe that his surviving family members, his friends, or his fellow Marines would want to relive their anguish and heartbreak? Who was I to tell their story?

I approached Timothy Fitzmaurice's sisters, Ellen Shea and Maureen Schiesser, with much trepidation about an idea for a book on their long lost brother. They had only met me one time in a passing social setting, so the idea that they would entrust the precious story of their brother's life to me seemed presumptuous. They graciously listened to my vision for the book, and then asked for some time to contemplate the idea. Ellen and Maureen needed to decide if they wanted to go back and unlock those places deep within themselves where the story of their brother's death had resided for more than four decades. After they courageously agreed to the book project, I moved outward from the immediate family to approach the other people who knew and loved and remembered Timothy Fitzmaurice.

What began to immediately emerge from everyone I contacted was an intense desire to talk about Tim, to talk about the memories of living with the Vietnam War, and to consider how those times shaped their entire lives. The overwhelming emotion was that it was *time*. It was time to come to grips with the past, and time to heal. A common theme ran through so many of my conversations and interviews. They had never really discussed, in depth, the true impact that Tim Fitzmaurice's life had had on their own lives. They had also never put words to the reality of having to live every day with the abiding presence of Vietnam.

Their lives were slower now. They had raised their families and were moving into retirement. I believed it to be the optimal time for them to reflect on how the death of a 20-year old in Vietnam, so long ago, had such a profound effect on the rest of their lives. How would things have been different had Timothy Fitzmaurice made it home from Vietnam?

Yes, there were days when I wondered if asking all of them to tell their stories was the right thing to do. But when they began to talk of Tim, or they went back to Vietnam in their minds and they spoke of what might have been, their feelings and emotions would come to the surface. When they told their stories of love and friendship, of romance and heartache, of longing and wonder, and all the possibilities of lives lived with Tim, instead of lives without him, I became comfortable with a story that had to be told.

At its heart, this book is about brotherhood in all its manifestations; the unwavering familial bond of love between siblings; the intense devotion of friendship in its fullest expression; and the steadfast covenant shared by those who risk their lives together on the field of battle. When the ties of brotherhood are tragically severed by the brutalities of war, the impact is enduring and overwhelming -- families are shattered, neighborhoods are fragmented, cities mourn, and a country's identity is forever altered.

More that 58,000 Americans never made it back alive from Vietnam. All of them had brave

PREFACE

family and friends waiting at home for their return, only to have their lives torn apart after receiving the news that their loved ones had been killed. Tim Fitzmaurice's older sister, Ellen, spoke of May 9, 1968, the day her brother was killed in Vietnam, as the day that changed all of her family members' lives forever. Tim's younger sister, Maureen, remembered Tim as someone who carried a special presence that naturally drew people to him -- he was a light within the family. This is a story of those left behind when a light is extinguished, and how they spent the rest of their lives trying to move forward out of the darkness.

CHAPTER ONE
FOUNDATION

"There's a shitload of gooks up here!" Those were the words that came back on the radio to Captain Frank Pacello, commanding officer of Mike Company, Third Battalion, Fifth Marine Regiment of the First Marine Division (Mike 3/5), after he had asked for a situation report on what the lead element in his unit had discovered. Those were the words uttered by Corporal Jerry Lomax that turned a "milk run," as Lomax referred to their previously uneventful patrol, into a five-day battle for the Marines' very survival. An undersized company of 90 men had stumbled into the middle of a North Vietnamese Army base camp with facilities for over 600 enemy soldiers. Previous intelligence reports had led the Marines of Mike 3/5 to believe that their mission was going to be uneventful, with no reported enemy activity in the immediate area.

No enemy activity -- that would have been good news for Lance Corporal Timothy Fitzmaurice. Tim had only been in Vietnam for about six weeks and was still getting acclimated to the harsh life of a combat Marine. Before this particular patrol, Tim had recently finished writing a letter to his girlfriend, Cindy Koenig, back in Chicago telling her that it may have been a mistake volunteering for duty in Vietnam. Tim's unit, Mike 3/5, had been seeing almost continuous combat since the start of the Tet Offensive, more than two months prior to Tim's arrival in Vietnam.

The extent of the fighting in Vietnam was well known to the Fitzmaurice family in Chicago. Tim's parents, Michael and Lubitza Fitzmaurice, his grandparents, Ilija and Anna Soraich, his brother, Jack, and his sisters, Ellen and Maureen, scoured the nightly news and the daily newspapers for any word on the fighting in Vietnam. Especially close attention was paid to reports of Marine Corps activity, and any possible mention of Tim's unit. Visits from the mailman were also eagerly awaited, because letters from Tim were the family's lifeline to hear how things were progressing for him in Vietnam.

Life overseas in a combat zone was not an experience that was unfamiliar to Tim's father, Michael. A World War II veteran of General George

S. Patton's Third Army, Michael Fitzmaurice had seen the horrors of war up close and was under no illusions about the dangers that his son was facing in Vietnam.

Michael Fitzmaurice was born the son of Irish immigrants in Chicago on July 13, 1905. Michael was the third of nine children born to Timothy and Ellen (Sheahan) Fitzmaurice. The Fitzmaurice family had settled in Holy Family Parish on Chicago's west side. Holy Family Church is the second oldest Roman Catholic church in Chicago. Spared from the ravages of the Great Chicago Fire in 1871, Holy Family Church went on to become a beacon of hope to the multitudes of Irish immigrants streaming into Chicago at the turn of the twentieth century. The west side of Chicago was a rough-and-tumble area of the city with widespread poverty being its prevailing characteristic.

The brutal realities of hard economic times forced the Irish immigrants to lean heavily on their Catholic faith for sustenance. Their local Catholic parish became central to the lives of these newly-arrived Chicagoans. The parish met their spiritual needs, but it also served other significant functions. Michael Fitzmaurice's grade school, Precious Blood, was attached to Holy Family Parish. The school provided not only instruction in the Catholic faith, but also a solid education in the secular subjects. Parish priests were not simply religious figures and teachers, they also acted as counselors and social workers. Parish events and meetings became the social fabric of the Irish family, and these gatherings would eventually lay the organizational groundwork for the incredibly successful entry of Irish immigrants into Chicago politics.

SMILE ON YOUR BROTHER

Michael Fitzmaurice

Life was exceedingly hard for Michael Fitzmaurice's family. After Michael finished his grade school years at Precious Blood there were no plans for him to continue his formal education. There were mouths to feed at home, and it was incumbent on Michael to begin contributing to the family finances. He worked a variety of odd jobs in an effort to bring home any money that he could to help support his seven brothers and one sister. He took respite from his trying days by enjoying some of the simpler pleasures in life. The Irish have always been great storytellers and, oftentimes, would enhance their gift for stirring narratives with song. Michael would come home from his daily grind, and regale his family with fantastic tales of what he had seen and done that day. Of course, no storytelling performance would be complete without a song or two for a strong finish. The harsh years, making his way in life on the rough streets of Chicago's west side, passed wearily for Michael. He eventually found steady employment working as a driver for O'Brien Brothers Coal Company. Delivering truckloads of coal for use in heating Chicago homes exposed Michael to tremendous amounts of coal dust. He would come home at the end of each workday with his skin and clothes covered in filthy blackness. This prolonged exposure to coal dust would eventually lead to an early misdiagnosis later in his life of Black Lung Disease. Michael settled into an exhaustive routine that sustained him for years, until the day he met the woman who would change the course of his life's journey.

Lubitza Soraich was born in Chicago on April 30, 1920. Her mother, Anna, was a Slovakian immigrant, and her father, Ilija, was an immigrant of Serbian descent. Lubitza had a sister, Militza, and a brother, Alex, and all were fluent in the Slovak language. The Soraich family settled on the northwest side of Chicago. Young Lubitza was a very outgoing, artistic, and athletic girl. Early family life for Lubitza was greatly influenced by the Sokol Movement. Sokol was a youth sports and gymnastics organization first founded by Miroslav Tyre and Jundrich Fugner in the city of Prague in what was then called Austria-Hungary in 1862. Primarily a fitness training center, the Sokol organization provided lectures, discussions, and group outings that were viewed as physical, moral, and intellectual training for the nation. This training extended to members of all classes, and, unique for the times, also extended to women. The movement spread across all regions populated by the Slavic culture including Poland, Serbia, Bulgaria, Russia, Slovenia, and Croatia. In many of these nations, the organization also served as the precursor of the Scout Movement. By 1937, American Sokol membership rolls counted nearly 20,000 adults, with Chicago chapters being some of the strongest in the nation. The organization's motto was, "A sound mind is a sound body," and Anna and Ilija Soraich made sure that their daughter, Lubitza, along with their other children, Alex and Militza, were very active participants. Like their Irish immigrant counterparts, Anna and Ilija were not shy about entering the fray of the Chicago political landscape. Chicago was, and is today, a city of neighborhoods, parishes, and ethnic enclaves. If you wanted representation, and your voice to be heard, you had to go out and do the hard work of community organizing. Ilija Soraich took to the Chicago way of doing things, eventually rising to the rank of precinct captain for his neighborhood. His job was to be the liaison between his immigrant neighbors and the political powers that ran the city. If someone was having a problem in the community, or if a person needed a particular favor done, Ilija would intervene on that person's behalf. In return, Ilija was entrusted to get out the vote to ensure reelection of the favored politician.

Lubitza Soraich Fitzmaurice

SMILE ON YOUR BROTHER

Grandpa and Grandma -
Ilija and Anna Soraich

Lubitza Soraich was brought up adhering to the tenets of the Serbian Orthodox faith. The Serbian Orthodox Church is one of the self-headed, independent, Orthodox Christian churches. The church was initially organized and located primarily in Serbia, Bosnia, and Croatia, but since the advent of widespread Serbian migration, there are now Serbian Orthodox communities worldwide.

Lubitza was born and raised in the same house where she would eventually raise her own children. It was a modest, two-story home located at 4740 North Kewanee Avenue in Chicago. The northwest side neighborhood was another ethnic area of the city, heavily populated by Eastern European families. Occasional train rides to downtown Chicago would be highlights during Lubitza's childhood. Staring at the elaborate window displays of the large department stores allowed young Lubitza to imagine places and things that were beyond her current existence. She was transported, if only for a little while, out of the reality of her day-to-day life to places where her dreams could live. She was especially close with her sister Militza, sharing a bedroom and talking late into the night about their plans and hopes for the future.

Lubitza Soraich attended Theodore Roosevelt High School in Chicago and graduated in 1938. Foregoing college after graduation, Lubitza took various small jobs to try to supplement the family income, and on the weekends she would head back downtown to do some shopping or visit a museum with her sister and friends. Tall and striking, she was frequently the object of interest of many a wishful suitor. She happened to be approached one day by an older gentleman who nimbly struck up a conversation with her. He was fifteen years her senior and possessed with an unmistakable sense of Irish wit and charm. Michael Fitzmaurice was immediately smitten with young Lubitza. To say they made an odd couple for the tenor of the times was an understatement. Lubitza was twenty years old, a child of Serbian and Slovak parents, and an adherent to the Serbian Orthodox faith. Michael was thirty-five years of age, and Irish Catholic to his core. An unlikely pairing to be sure, but it was love that quickly closed the cultural gap. These were serious times that Lubitza and Michael were living through. The war in Europe was now almost two years old, and there was a feeling of inevitability that America's entrance into the conflict was a foregone certainty. Their courtship moved along rapidly, but was violently interrupted by the events of December 7, 1941. The attack on the American naval base at Pearl Harbor, Hawaii, had thrust the United States into World War II, and all able-bodied men were heading to their local recruiting offices to sign up in service of their country. Even though he was then thirty-six years of age, there was never any question that Michael would be doing his part for the war effort. Within four months of the attack on Pearl Harbor, Michael had volunteered for the Army and would be leaving for Basic Training. Life was getting serious now and required thoughtful consideration in planning for the future. Michael and Lubitza were in love, and had decided to wait for each other until after the war. If Michael could make it back to Lubitza, they would marry and begin their dreams together.

The horrendous loss of life for American service personnel required that Michael Fitzmaurice's training be accelerated in order to facilitate his entry into a frontline Army unit. Michael ended up under the command of General George S. Patton in Patton's Third Army fighting in North Africa.

In November of 1942, the first ever British-American amphibious invasion landed three separate task forces on the African continent, and quickly seized key parts of French North Africa. Once ashore, troops linked up with the advancing British Eighth Army. Five months of hard fighting against German General Erwin Rommel's vaunted *Afrika*

Korps desert veterans awaited American troops. From the beginning, the operation faced problems with logistical hurdles, inexperienced troops, and ill-trained staff officers. General Patton was brought in to lead the operation after a poorly performing corps commander, General Lloyd Fredenhall, was replaced by Supreme Allied Commander, General Dwight D. Eisenhower. General Patton wasted no time in injecting his iron will onto his new troops. Patton biographer Martin Blumenson put it bluntly, "Patton had to be ruthless. He had only a short time to shake his troops out of their slovenly habits and into a state of readiness." The newly-arrived general believed that the division commanders that he had inherited from Fredenhall's command lacked the aforementioned ruthlessness, and, in Patton's view, were oversensitive about casualties. It was the application of General Patton's callous and merciless ways that caused Michael Fitzmaurice to come to despise the man. Patton held a "victory at all costs" mentality, even if those costs were tremendous amounts of American dead and wounded. Michael's time under Patton's command came to an abrupt and terrifying end on February 12, 1943. Michael was seriously wounded by an exploding artillery shell. The force of the blast broke Michael's back, while shrapnel from the exploding shell embedded itself in Michael's upper chest and neck area. Information from the battlefield moved exceedingly slowly in 1943, and it was several weeks before Michael's family, and Lubitza, would be informed of his serious condition. By the time of the release of the news, Michael was already back in a stateside hospital in Battle Creek, Michigan. The hospital stay in Battle Creek proved to be an extensive one, as Michael had to remain under care there for a full year recuperating from his wounds. After his lengthy term in the hospital, Michael went home from Battle Creek with permanent reminders of all that he had endured. There were shrapnel fragments lodged in his neck, that doctors deemed too risky to go in to remove.

FOUNDATION

Lubitza Soraich and Michael Fitzmaurice
pictured before Michael left home
for service in World War II.

During his hospital stay, Michael was sustained by letters from Lubitza and stories of life back in Chicago. He longed to return to her and the life they knew before the war. Michael used his desire for home, and a return to Lubitza, as motivation during his long and arduous recuperation and rehabilitation. He would hope and pray that things could be as before, but there was no mistaking the physical and mental scars that Michael had brought back with him. After taking the time to renew their courtship, and to get to know one another again, Michael and Lubitza made plans to be wed.

One minor stumbling block impeded their way to the altar. It was imperative for Michael that any children brought forth from a marriage to Lubitza be raised in the Roman Catholic faith. Additionally, while it was not a strict necessity that Lubitza convert to Roman Catholicism in order to raise the children as Catholics, it would make things easier. So, for love and family and faith in their future together, Lubitza converted to Catholicism. She would come to embrace that faith with the zeal that only a truly committed convert could bring to the endeavor. On April 7, 1945, at Chicago's City Hall, Michael Fitzmaurice and Lubitza Soraich became husband and wife.

The newlywed couple took up residence directly above Lubitza's parents, Ilija and Anna Soraich, on the second floor of the home on Kewanee Avenue. Michael resumed his work as a coal truck driver for the O'Brien Brothers Company, and the young couple immediately threw themselves into parish life at Saint Edward Church. They volunteered at many of the parish's social activities. Michael joined the Saint Edward Holy Name Society, working to aid the sick and poor throughout the local community. Lubitza became a member of the Saint Anne's Sodality, a parish organization open to married women, with a special focus on strengthening devotion to the Catholic faith through charitable work.

SMILE ON YOUR BROTHER

Saint Edward Church became the spiritual home for Michael and Lubitza. It would be the place where they would celebrate some of their most cherished family memories, and it would also become the place of refuge they would turn to when the cold realities of life came inevitably to their door.

The Fitzmaurice family home at 4740 North Kewanee Street in Chicago

It wasn't long before Michael and Lubitza had a new mouth to feed, with the birth of their first child, a daughter, Ellen, on June 20, 1946. Not long after came the birth of their son, Timothy. Tim was born on January 6, 1948, and one year later, son Jack arrived on January 21, 1949. It would be almost nine years before daughter Maureen rounded out the Fitzmaurice clan with her birth on November 6, 1957. Saint Edward Parish was witness to all of the family's central activities that came with growing up Catholic in Chicago in the 1950s. Baptisms, first holy communions, confirmations, graduations -- it was all part of the gradual march to adulthood for the Fitzmaurice family. In 1950s Chicago, it was the parish that was the character, the descriptor, that gave Catholic Chicagoans their identity. Saint Edward was interwoven into the fiber of the Fitzmaurice family, and it was matriarch Lubitza's converted Catholic devotion that cemented that identity. Together, always, with the young family were Grandpa and

Grandma Soraich, supporting and loving grandparents, continually doing whatever they could to ease the stresses on their daughter's growing brood. Money was always tight, so there were not opportunities for family vacations or summer trips. The large back yard became the family sanctuary. Ellen Fitzmaurice Shea remembered the family yard, "We knew that we had the best backyard in the world and we loved it very much. It became a gathering place for all of our friends." Lubitza's brother, Alex Soraich, recalled a particularly funny episode that took place in the family yard. "Tim and Jack loved to go camping, setting up a tent in their own back yard. One night they invited my son, Bryan, to camp out with them. It was a very cold night, but the boys decided they could handle the elements with no trouble. Jack was the first to wake up and leave the tent to come back inside the house. Tim was right behind him. They left my son outside in the cold until Grandma Soraich went out there to rescue him. Tim and Jack got a big laugh out of that one."

The Fitzmaurice children in the family yard. (L to R) Jack, Maureen, Ellen, and Timothy.

Young Tim Fitzmaurice was growing quickly. He followed the usual path of Catholic boys at the time. School activities, sports, altar boy service, and, in the true Sokol tradition, he would grow to develop a keen interest in scouting. Saint Edward

Parish was very big in promoting membership and activity in scouting. The Boy Scouts gave Tim an opportunity to develop individual skills and foster his own identity. He especially enjoyed the extended summer camping excursions at a Michigan scouting reservation as a chance to get away from home and experience new things. Scout leader and Fitzmaurice family friend, Jim Heinlein, recalled those carefree days. "Every year we took Boy Scout Troop 904 on an extended summer excursion to Owasippe Scout Reservation near Whitehall, Michigan. We would settle in at Camp Beard and instruct the boys in swimming, fishing, boating, and horseback riding -- basically how to survive in the great outdoors. I remember Tim trying to make himself a pancake breakfast over an open campfire. He took the pancake batter and poured it into the frying pan, filling the entire pan with batter. I asked Tim how he was planning on flipping that huge pancake when it was time to cook the other side. He told me that he would simply cut the pancake in half so it would be easy to flip. I then suggested that maybe he should cut the pancake in four pieces to make it even easier to deal with. He looked at me with that sly grin of his and he said, 'I don't think I can eat four pieces. I'm not that hungry'. Tim had such a great sense of humor."

The final night of the camping trips to Owasippe would always end with Tim, and the rest of his Scout troop, sitting around a fire, singing their traditional camp song. The lyrics harkened back to a simpler time: "Look ahead to the days of summer, look ahead to the freedom that it gives. We'll return one day to Camp Beard, where the spirit of scouting lives."

By the spring of 1962, Tim Fitzmaurice was approaching decision time for his choice of high schools, and the school selection that he would eventually make brought him into contact with new friends - friends who would laugh with him, friends who would love him, friends who would go to war with him, and friends who would wait for his return.

CHAPTER TWO
REVELATION

"Let every nation know, whether it wishes us well or ill, that we shall pay any price, bear any burden, meet any hardship, support any friend, oppose any foe, in order to assure the survival and success of liberty." In the autumn of 1962, members of the baby-boom generation were entering their high school years. Inspired by the words of their new president, John F. Kennedy, America's young people were moving out from the protection of their homes and parents and forging their own way in the world. Tempered by the seriousness of the times, but bolstered by the guiding compass of the call of President Kennedy to "ask not what your country can do for you, ask what you can do for your country," this new generation would begin their path to adulthood.

DePaul Academy High School was opened as an all-boys prep school to DePaul University on September 5, 1898, and located on Chicago's north side, in the city's Lincoln Park neighborhood. The namesake of the school was Saint Vincent de Paul (1581-1660), who was the founder of the Congregation of the Mission, a religious community whose members, the Vincentian Priests of the Western Province, helped establish the school. The school's enrollment peak was in 1960 when it reached 850 students.

REVELATION

DePaul Academy High School
in Chicago, Illinois.

Tim Fitzmaurice began his high school career at DePaul Academy in the fall of 1962. Roger McGill, a Fitzmaurice family friend from Saint Edward Parish, summed up his neighborhood's high school choice selection process pretty simply by stating that "the good boys went to DePaul Academy, the bad boys went to the public high school."

The creed of the Vincentian Fathers, who presided over the classrooms at DePaul Academy, was to prepare young men for manhood through hard work and discipline. Freshman year was a time of great transition for Tim Fitzmaurice. Life on Kewanee Avenue was starting to become a bit stifling. Emerging health problems, related to the onset of emphysema, and the lingering effects of the complications from his war wounds, had seriously slowed the physical abilities of Tim's father, Michael. It would not be long before Michael had to stop working altogether, forced to spend significant amounts of time resting at home. Lubitza was working full-time at a local insurance agency to pay the family bills. Tim's sister, Ellen Fitzmaurice, was attending high school at Alvernia High School, an all-girls Catholic institution, and was busy working when not attending classes. By the autumn of 1963, Jack Fitzmaurice had followed his brother, Tim, to DePaul Academy, while their sister, four-year-old Maureen, remained at home.

After the initial adjustment period of the first few weeks at DePaul Academy, Tim settled into high school life quite well. His outgoing personality and infectious laughter allowed him to make friends very easily, and his class work and grades were excellent. He especially enjoyed utilizing his problem-solving and analytical skills to excel in math class.

Much of the incoming enrollment at DePaul Academy came directly from the nearby Catholic grade school, Saint Vincent de Paul. Almost all of Tim's newfound friends were boys from the Lincoln Park neighborhood adjacent to DePaul Academy. There was Len Swiatly, the oldest child in a family that would eventually reach nine children. Len played freshman football and ran cross-country with Tim. The cross-country experiment, however, didn't turn out so well for Tim. Len remembered, "Tim was six feet tall, and he was the slowest person in the world. We were having track practice one afternoon down near Diversey Harbor on the lakefront. We had to run around this huge field at the conclusion of the race. Tim decided that he would try to cut across the field in order to pass everybody to win the race. Everyone saw what he was trying to do and sped up. Tim cut out a huge part of the race and still came in last. It was hilarious."

Danny Boyle lived just a short walk down the street from DePaul Academy. Danny remembered

Tim as the "sparkplug of our group." "He was the one who was always coming up with the ideas of what to do. Of course, it helped that he was the only one who had a car. His Mom had won some kind of used car and by Tim's sophomore year he was driving it to school every day, and driving us around in it every night."

Bryan Dillon was the oldest child in a family that would ultimately grow to thirteen children. Len Swiatly's family and Bryan's family once shared the same address, with the Dillon's occupying the second floor and the Swiatly's living above them on the third floor of a three-flat apartment building. The Dillon's later moved down the street, with their growing family rapidly filling a home not far from DePaul Academy. Tim and Bryan hit it off right away. The first-born sons of hard-working first generation Irish-American, and World War II veteran fathers, Tim and Bryan had much in common. They, too, were on the cross-country team together, and Tim even tried to get Bryan to come out and join him on the DePaul Academy football team. "That lasted one day," Bryan said.

Bryan's father, Bob Dillon, had sweet, emotional memories of his son's friendship with Tim. "Tim and Bryan were always together," Bob recalled. "Some of my fondest memories of Tim were from Christmas mornings." Lubitza Fitzmaurice was a wonderful baker. She would rise very early on Christmas Day to make incredible holiday cookies. But it was Lubitza's special recipe apple and cheese strudel that was her pride and joy. After the goodies were fresh out of the oven, Lubitza would send her son, Tim, over to the Dillon house to deliver the Christmas treats. "We'd be enjoying the delicious food that Tim had brought over for us, while Tim would be busy looking underneath the Christmas tree, Bob continued. "He would be checking out the toys that all of the kids had received. He'd always pick one out for his favorite and start to play with it." Bob Dillon was 88 years old now and sitting in his family room in the same house that he and his wife, Pat, have lived in for over 60 years. He pointed in the general direction of his living room, to the spot where the Christmas tree had always stood. His eyes welled up with tears, "I can still see Tim over there like it was yesterday."

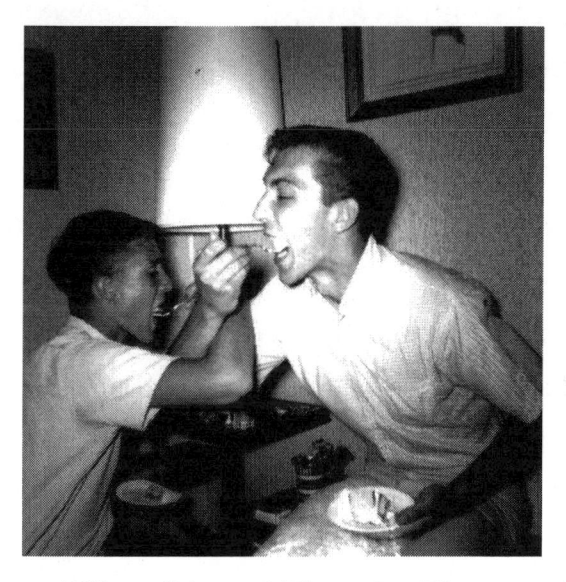

Bryan Dillon (L) and Timothy Fitzmaurice enjoying birthday cake at Cindy Koenig's 16th birthday party.

The Vietnam War was a couple of years away and, for Tim and his friends, there was still time to be young. Len Swiatly remembered the friends' first experience drinking together. They were in Len's basement and one of the boys had brought a bottle of scotch. While passing the bottle around, they quickly realized that no one could handle the taste of the alcohol, so they sent Len upstairs to see if there was anything to mix with the scotch in order to make it drinkable. Len came back downstairs with the only thing he could find --Tang. The scotch and Tang party ended prematurely, however, when Len's parents came home unexpectedly and caught the boys drinking. Len laughed when he recalled that "they all got away with it, but I was grounded for a month. Such good Catholic boys we were."

Around the same time period, Tim had also developed a keen interest in kayaking. He and an older boy he befriended from the DePaul neighborhood, Bill Keglewitsch, constructed a kayak in the Fitzmaurice family yard. The two budding sailors made a wooden frame and stretched canvas over the wood. They then sprayed the kayak frame with fiberglass before putting the finishing touches on it with beautiful red and white paint.

"That kayak was used quite a bit by Timmy," Ellen Fitzmaurice Shea recalled. "Mom would drive him down to Diversey Harbor where he could launch it. It seems to me that everyone got a chance to go out on Lake Michigan in that kayak. One time Timmy took another neighbor, Bobby Buschbacker, out on the lake. They were letting themselves rest after some time on the water, but the kayak began drifting toward an area of the lake where there was a shooting range. Timmy told us how the two of them had to paddle quickly to get away from the tiny splashes in the water near them. He said that they had left a huge wake behind them while moving away from that shooting range."

Bryan Dillon reminisced on a touching and funny adventure that he and Tim shared. "Tim had made a two-man kayak and we took it down to Lincoln Park lagoon for one of its first voyages. We were on the water trying to familiarize ourselves with the safe and proper operation of the kayak. It wasn't too long before we realized that we were in over our heads, literally, when the kayak flipped over on us in the middle of the lagoon. We had to swim back to the shoreline, pulling the kayak behind us. It was a little embarrassing. I lost my glasses when the kayak tipped and had to tell my dad that my glasses were at the bottom of the lagoon --he was not happy. Tim and I never did get another chance to take the kayak out together."

Tim Fitzmaurice's partner in the initial construction of the beloved kayak, Bill Keglewitsch, was drafted into the United States Army in early 1966. Before leaving for boot camp he reminded his young friend that the kayak was now Tim's to care for until Bill was able to make it back home. In September of 1966, Bill Keglewitsch began his tour of duty in Vietnam. He served honorably with the Army's 27th Maintenance Battalion of the 1st Cavalry Division. Corporal Keglewitsch's main responsibility consisted of repairing field radios. Nine months into his tour, on June 15, 1967, Bill Keglewitsch died in Vietnam of an undetermined illness. He was just twenty-three years old. His name stands proudly on the Vietnam Memorial Wall on Panel 21 E, Line 106.

With the financial situation at the Fitzmaurice house getting tighter every day, Tim took a job with Niedermaier Design, doing silkscreen work and decorating store windows. The firm's owner was Dale Niedermaier. Dale brought Tim under his wing, and took great pride in introducing Tim to the ins and outs of the design and decorating trade. Dale was drawn to Tim's engaging personality and was impressed with Tim's enthusiasm for the company. Mr. Niedermaier quickly seized on Tim's obvious creative and artistic talents. It wasn't long before he was incorporating some of Tim's design ideas into the firm's work. Dale became confident in handing more and more responsibilities to Tim, especially during the Christmas season when the volume of the company's design work was at its highest level. Tim used the opportunity of his ever-increasing work load to ask Dale to hire Bryan Dillon to assist on projects. Together, the best friends would work late into the evenings, after store hours, to complete decorations of department store windows in downtown Chicago. Dale Niedermaier became a mentor to Tim, sharing his business acumen, but also imparting some of his life wisdom on a young man who was beginning to formulate some serious thoughts as to what the future would hold for him.

Cindy Koenig Moderi was born and raised in Saint Clement Parish, just a few blocks from DePaul Academy. Her father worked for the city of Chicago in the Water Department and her mother worked for the Chicago Tribune. "It was your typical 1950s Catholic upbringing," Cindy recalled. "Catholic grade school and then on to the all-girls Catholic high school. We didn't have many chances to interact with boys our age. We had to look for certain events to go to, and then hope that some of the boys from the neighboring high schools would be there, too. Saint Bonaventure was a nearby parish to Saint Clement, and they held a carnival in the fall of 1964. I was there with some of my friends and saw this very tall boy in a black golf shirt. He was so cute." It wasn't until December 26, 1964, that Tim and Cindy had their first date. "Tim invited me to a dance and said that he would pick me up in his car. He was one year older than I was and he had a car, so it was a pretty big deal for me. The car was an old aqua and white model that his mother had won in a contest. Tim wanted the car looking extra nice for our first date, so he put the car through a car wash before coming over to pick me up. After he had come in and sat down for a while to meet my parents, we went out to the car to go to the dance. But we couldn't get in the car because the door locks had frozen with the water from the car wash. Tim was so embarrassed, but with my Dad's help we were able to get the doors opened so we could make the dance. You know, I still have the dress from that first date."

Cindy Koenig Moderi

Three months before Tim had met Cindy, the United States Congress passed, almost unanimously, legislation called the Tonkin Gulf Resolution. President Lyndon B. Johnson signed the resolution on August 10, 1964, allowing the United States to take conventional military action against the forces of North Vietnam "to promote the maintenance of international peace and security in Southeast Asia." After years of providing indirect help to the South Vietnamese government against the Vietcong, who were Communist rebels supported by the North Vietnamese regime of Ho Chi Minh, the United States had directly entered the conflict. Vietnam was 10,000 miles away from Chicago, but it was getting closer by the day.

"We didn't talk about the war early on," Bryan Dillon remembered. "It was so far away and we were busy with everything that we had going on back then. But as we moved closer to our graduation date in 1966 things changed."

The Vietnam War had been escalating rapidly since the signing of the Tonkin Gulf Resolution. On

REVELATION

March 8, 1965, the United States Marines landed on the beaches of Danang, South Vietnam. Their mission, ostensibly, was to secure the American air base in Danang. The Marines were under the command of Brigadier General Frederick Karch. Prior to the Marines' landing, General Karch had told reporters that the activities of his men would be strictly defined as a defensive posture to protect American assets. General Wallace Greene, Jr., Commandant of the Marine Corps, wasn't quite so diplomatic, however. General Greene was quoted as saying, "Our assignment is to defend that big complex at Danang, but you can't defend a place like that by sitting on your ditty-box. You've got to go out and aggressively patrol. And that's what our people are doing. And the one thing that I emphasized to them while I was out there was to find these Vietcong and kill them." Thirty five hundred Marines came ashore that March, and by the end of 1965 there would be 200,000 U.S. troops in Vietnam.

As Tim Fitzmaurice began his senior year at DePaul Academy, the Vietnam War hit home in a tragic way. On September 6, 1965, Lance Corporal Michael Terrance Badsing, Charlie Company, First Battalion, Ninth Marine Regiment of the Third Marine Division, was the first boy from Saint Edward Parish to be killed in Vietnam. Mike Badsing was born and raised just a few blocks from Tim's home. He attended grammar school at Saint Edward, and then went on to the local public high school. Mike was the first Marine from Chicago to be killed in action, and his death sent shock waves throughout Tim's neighborhood. Mike Badsing was remembered by Philip Pavone, a brother Marine who served with him in Vietnam: "Mike was a true blue Marine, he loved the Marine Corps. There is no greater love than a man who lays down his life for his fellow Marines. He taught me everything on how to be a good Marine, and because of that he saved my life, and the lives of a lot of other Marines. Mike is my hero, and I miss him very much."

REVELATION

Timothy Fitzmaurice in his graduation photo from DePaul Academy.

The entire community turned out for Mike Badsing's funeral at Saint Edward Church. Unfortunately, Mike's flag-draped casket would not be the last to arrive at the steps of Saint Edward from the killing fields of Vietnam. The war had come home, and gone were the first three carefree years of high school for Tim Fitzmaurice and his friends. Those years gave way to a senior year filled with life-altering decisions. "We were growing up in a hurry," Bryan Dillon said.

CHAPTER THREE
RESOLUTION

"Our dads had fought in World War II, and we just figured that this was our turn, our war." That's how Bryan Dillon put it when remembering how he and Tim were feeling as they approached graduation day from DePaul Academy. "You have to understand, we knew we were going to be drafted anyway -- we weren't going to have a choice. That's just the way it was back then."

The draft, or Selective Service as it was more formally known, was in full operation in the summer of 1966. "You can't comprehend the looming feeling of helplessness that the inevitability of being drafted had over us," said Tim Fitzmaurice's good friend, Len Swiatly. "Especially for those of us who weren't considering college right away. It was coming, and there was no way around it." The draft, and all the inequities that were associated with it, would be one of the most divisive issues throughout the war in Vietnam. The elaborate system of deferments, the ability of the well-connected to achieve highly sought after slots in the military Reserves or National Guard, and the dubious nature of fit-for-duty classifications, all contributed to the contempt that many citizens had for the fairness of the Selective Service system and its implementation.

Tim Fitzmaurice wasn't waiting to be drafted, however. He was going to take control over his situation by serving his country on his own terms, and for Tim that meant volunteering for enlistment in the United States Marine Corps Reserves. Tim's high school friend from St. Edward Parish, Paul Pennick, remembered those days, "Tim and I were looking to get into the Coast Guard, the National Guard, or any Reserve branch that would take us. We didn't want to be drafted. But this was Chicago in May of 1966 -- none of those service branches had any openings. All of those coveted slots went to the well-connected. A guy I worked with told us to try the Marine Corps Reserves. At the time, I didn't even know that the Marines had Reserves. I thought it was strange that the they were able to sign us up right away. Once we arrived in San Diego, and got our first taste of Marine Corps boot camp, I realized why there were slots available in the Marines. We were so young and naïve."

"He didn't talk about his plans with anyone from the family," Tim's sister, Ellen, recalled. "I remember that Uncle Alex, my mother's brother, was in the Marines during World War II, but I don't really think that had any influence on Timmy's decision to join. He just went ahead on his own and signed up. There was no discussion with my parents beforehand as I remember." For Tim's younger sister, Maureen, there was always a lingering question as to just exactly why Tim signed up when he did. "My father got really sick when I was in the second grade, and Tim left for the Marines when I was starting third grade. I often wondered if there was a connection between his enlistment and Dad's illness. Did he think that one less mouth to feed at home would be easier for my Mom? It wasn't. His leaving changed my Mom."

By the time Tim joined the Marine Corps, he and Cindy Koenig had been going steady for over a year - a lifetime for a high school senior and his 17 year-old girlfriend. "I was doing Tim's term papers during his final year of high school. He was working long hours late into the evenings for Niedermaier Design, so it didn't leave him enough time to focus on his schoolwork. I think he knew that college was not going to be a part of his immediate plans, but I also think that he wasn't really sure what to do next. I believe that the indecision that he felt, more than anything, left him vulnerable to his final decision to join the Marines."

Tim Fitzmaurice left for Marine Corps boot camp on June 16, 1966. Paul Pennick was with Tim at the Marine Corps Recruit Depot in San Diego, California. "Tim and I went to boot camp together. The Marine recruiter who originally signed us up in Chicago had promised that we would stay together all during our training, but as soon as we got to boot camp we were put in different platoons. We were able to see each other for Catholic Mass on Sundays. Those were the greatest Masses that I've ever attended, because it was the only time during our training when we had any quiet time. The rest of the week we would be getting screamed at constantly by our drill instructors, but for an hour on Sundays we had that time for ourselves and I was able to talk with Tim. It was at Mass where Tim told me that he had changed his mind, and he was now going to join the regular Marines. I started yelling at him and telling him, not very nicely, how crazy he was to do that. They were constantly putting pressure on the reservists to sign up for the regular Marines, and Tim was always trying to please people, so I think that was a big factor on why he signed on to the active duty Marine Corps. You know, Tim was such a sweet and generous guy. When you're young, you don't appreciate having someone like that in your life, but as you get older you realize how special, and unique, that those types of people really are, and you miss everything that your life could have been had you had a lifelong friend like that. I think about him often and I miss him."

RESOLUTION

Timothy Fitzmaurice and Cindy Koenig before the DePaul Academy senior prom of 1966.

Around that same time, Tim Fitzmaurice's eventual unit, the Third Battalion, Fifth Marine Regiment of the First Marine Division, had made its initial deployment to Vietnam in the ever-widening war. Troop levels in Vietnam had gone from 200,000 at the end of 1965 to 385,000 at the end of 1966. The war still held a majority of popular support at home. President Lyndon B. Johnson assured the American people that the United States was putting a stop to communism in Indochina, and that the mission in Vietnam was winning over the hearts and minds of the South Vietnamese people.

Tim's boot camp experience consisted of ten weeks of recruit training, a rigorous trial of military indoctrination designed to turn civilians into Marines. Following boot camp, the new Marines would be put through eight weeks of Advanced Infantry Training. It was during this advanced training that the new Marines would get schooled on what to expect when they got to Vietnam. By the end of 1966, casualty figures showed that 7,900 Americans had been killed, and 37,000 more had been wounded up to that point in the war.

Marine Corps training passed quickly for Tim without a break until Christmas of 1966. He was then given a very brief leave of absence for the Christmas holiday. Tim considered heading home to Chicago, but the travel cost was too prohibitive. So instead of spending Christmas alone at Camp Pendleton in San Diego, Tim purchased an inexpensive bus ticket to celebrate the holiday with his cousin, Janice Bowen, in Phoenix, Arizona. Janice was the daughter of Lubitza Fitzmaurice's sister, Militza. Militza Soraich had married a man by the name of Wallin Bowen, and began raising their family not far from Grandma and Grandpa Soraich's home in Chicago. Lubitza and Militza's children were brought up playing together in the back yard on Kewanee Avenue.

"Tim was a mischievous, energetic boy," Janice remembered. "Jack was much more moody, but very close to Tim. The family atmosphere was very strong, always centered on the guidance of Grandma and Grandpa. Grandpa especially saw himself in Tim; they resembled one another so much. By 1955, we had moved out to Phoenix, and had been living there ever since, when Tim came to spend his Christmas with us when he was on leave from the Marine Corps in 1966. Tim lit up the house when he came to see us. He had a great sense of humor and loved to sing songs. He was very creative, but I saw him as tender and vulnerable also. It had been a long time since I had seen him, and with his Marine Corps uniform on he was quite handsome. It was obvious that the Marine Corps had been successful with its training because he would sit in the kitchen with us and he was talking tough. He wasn't a tough guy, but he was saying things like he wanted to be the first guy on his block to go to Vietnam. He was also smoking cigarettes then and I think that he thought that added to his bravado. One of my fondest memories was when I took him out touring around Phoenix in my car. He was admiring the way that I was handling the car, I guess, because he told me 'you drive like a guy'. But underneath it all was this level of stress of what was to come. My fiancée at that time was already in Vietnam serving with the 101st Airborne Division, and I could tell by the letters home that he was sending that a different man would be coming home to me than the one who left for Vietnam. I worried about Tim, and the whole family, what was in store for him when it was his turn to go to Vietnam."

After finishing his advanced infantry training, the initial duty assignment was a fortunate one for Tim. He was not being sent to Vietnam. Instead he was sent to Guantanamo Bay, Cuba, to be part of the Marine Brigade that guarded the Naval Base there. While Tim was stationed at Guantanamo Bay, his eventual unit, the Fifth Marine Regiment, was in Vietnam throughout 1967, engaging in one murderous combat operation after another. The American casualties were staggeringly high all over Vietnam, and when the dead began returning home at an alarming rate, public sentiment started turning against the war.

Back in Saint Edward Parish, another family was making the long walk up the stairs of the church behind a casket. Private First Class John Earl Cronin of Echo Company, Second Battalion, First Marine Regiment of the First Marine Division, was killed on May 14, 1967, in Quang Nam Province in South Vietnam. Just 20 years old, John volunteered for the Marine Corps right out of high school. His sister, Nancy, remembered him: "John was my older brother and my friend. He played the trumpet and liked jazz and had his own pool cue. He was a cool older brother. He watched out for me and I still have a postcard that he sent to me from boot camp. Twenty is so very young to die -- what a future he might have had. His passing affected us all profoundly, and he will live in our hearts forever. When I think of him I remember his smile, and sometimes I can still hear his laugh. Rest in peace my brother and I'll see you again on the other side."

Vietnam was taking the best of a parish, a neighborhood, a city, and a country, and there were still so many more battles to fight, and so many more lives to be lost.

Tim and his girlfriend, Cindy Koenig, stayed connected while Tim was away. They exchanged frequent letters telling each other stories of their now very different lives. Cindy was a senior in high school and making preparations for college. She missed Tim terribly, and the letters sent back and forth between them always spoke of their future. He was going to serve out his time in the Marine Corps and return to her in Chicago, where they could begin to plan their lives together. As the last year of high school ended for Cindy, all of her other classmates were eagerly making arrangements for their biggest night of the year -- senior prom. The girls were getting together to exchange ideas about whom to bring to prom and what to wear, with excited plans on how the evening would turn out. Cindy's plans were different, however. Her date was on station in Guantanamo Bay, Cuba, so there would be no prom night for her. No dress, no corsage, no limousine, no dancing, no pictures, and no memories. On prom night, while the rest of her classmates were out celebrating their graduation, Cindy stayed home and wrote a letter to Tim. "I wasn't going to go to prom without him."

RESOLUTION

Timothy Fitzmaurice at the Marine Corps Recruit Depot, San Diego, California.

Tim Fitzmaurice remained on duty station at Guantanamo Bay throughout the summer of 1967. In October, he was given a leave to come home to Chicago. It had been over a year since he had seen Cindy. "I remember that leave like it was yesterday," Cindy said. "Tim had been away that whole year. I had graduated from high school in June, and Tim's mom got me a job working with her at Kemper Insurance. I met a guy at work and started dating him in August, but when Tim came home I realized that I really still loved him, so I immediately stopped seeing this guy from work. I told Tim about it all and then he broke up with me! It was a very bad night. A few days later, however, we agreed to go out with a few friends. I brought Tim's ring from the ring dance to return to him, but in the end he didn't want it back, because we both still felt the same about each other."

Tim's sister, Maureen, remembered the special treatment that a Marine received while he was home on leave. "Our family followed the Catholic 'no meat on Friday' rule pretty faithfully back then. Tim had convinced my Mom, however, that since he was an active duty Marine that he was granted special dispensation by the Pope, and that it was OK for him to have meat on Friday. That Friday night we all had buttered noodles and tuna fish sandwiches -- Tim had a Delmonico steak. When he was questioned by my Dad during dinner, Tim disclosed that he had stretched the truth just a little bit. The Pope had never given any such special dispensation for Marines. Tim simply wanted to have steak for dinner! My Dad was laughing, but my Mom was mortified. She thought that she was going to burn in hell for feeding Tim meat on a Friday. When Ellen came home from work that evening she just rolled her eyes when Tim told her the story. Tim couldn't stop laughing. I still remember Tim's laugh. He had a great laugh."

The leave was a great time for Tim. He was reconnecting with old friends, with Cindy, and with family. He was immensely proud of his service in the Marine Corps. He felt that he was really accomplishing something on a personal level. But as he left to head back to Guantanamo Bay, and the resumption of his duties, there was something that was bothering him. Inside he was becoming restless, believing that he was not fulfilling his real duties as a Marine. So many from his parish and neighborhood had already left for Vietnam, and somehow, Tim felt that he was being spared that particular test. He was determined to do something about that when he got back to Guantanamo Bay. First stop, though, on his way back to Cuba, was the Marine Corps Air Base at Cherry Point, North Carolina.

Neal Schilling was a Fitzmaurice family friend, a 1960 graduate of Saint Edward Grade School, and a 1964 graduate of DePaul Academy High

RESOLUTION

School. Neal was also a United States Marine returning from thirteen months of active duty in Vietnam when he ran into Tim Fitzmaurice at the Cherry Point Marine Air Base in the fall of 1967. "I was in the receiving barracks at Cherry Point and I spotted Tim right away. He had a torn T-shirt on because he had just been in a fight with another Marine. I gave him one of my extra shirts and we started talking. We had a nice long talk about life back home in Chicago, and the things that each of us had been doing during our time in the Corps. He finally got around to telling me about his dissatisfaction with his assignment at Guantanamo Bay, and that he was planning on putting in a request for duty in Vietnam. This really concerned me because I had just gotten back from my thirteen month tour over there, and I really did not like the way that the war was being fought. I didn't see any signs of us winning the war. Our units would fight and die for the same pieces of ground over and over again. It all seemed like such a waste to me. It wasn't what I had expected at all. I had volunteered for the Marines to go to Vietnam and do my part to win the war -- to fight battles, take ground, and move forward. I quickly found out that it wasn't like that. Our units would engage the enemy, not to take ground, but simply to kill more of them than they could kill of us. It was a waste of very good people, and I became disheartened at the futility of it all. I told all of this to Tim. But, of course, in the end, I knew it wouldn't do any good. Just as if someone had given me the same talk, I would have ignored it and gone on to volunteer for Vietnam. We're Marines -- that's what we're trained to do."

Tim Fitzmaurice may have been telling his friend, Neal Schilling, that his mind was made up about volunteering for Vietnam, but his letters home to his girlfriend, Cindy, were showing that he still had some trepidation on what the future might bring. Tim wrote Cindy on October 22, 1967,

RESOLUTION

"I've got less than 280 days left in the Corps now, too short, I hope, for 'Nam." This sentiment was in direct contradiction with what Tim had told his friend, Neal, just a week earlier at Cherry Point. To his fellow Marine, Tim Fitzmaurice was itching and ready to go to Vietnam. To his girlfriend, however, Tim's doubts and reservations could be more easily expressed. The internal conflicts that raged inside Tim were settled by the time of his follow-up letter to Cindy. On November 28, 1967, Tim wrote Cindy of his decision to request assignment to Vietnam. "There are many things in this world that I want, a good education, a good job, a family, and you. But not if other people have to die for it to be that way." Tim had decided to take his turn in Vietnam because of his loyalty to his brother Marines. He would go to war, and maybe in doing so, spare just one other Marine the need to do the same. Duty in Vietnam could have passed Tim by, and all of the dreams that he had planned with Cindy would not have to be put at risk. Love, family, friends, work, and the future of a 19-year-old all lay before him. It could all have begun in less than a year's time. Tim could have served out the rest of his enlistment without dealing with the uncertainty and danger of a combat tour in Vietnam. He could not claim that he didn't have a clarity of choice -- his conversation with Neal Schilling had given him that. Tim could never have been prepared for what awaited him in Vietnam, but he had been given enough information to realize the true gravity of his decision.

It was also in late November 1967, that Tim Fitzmaurice wrote to his parents of his determination to go to war. The timing of that letter could not have been more grievous for Michael and Lubitza. Tim's decision to go to Vietnam meant that the war was theirs now, and they were stricken with worry of what was to come. It had been only a few days prior to receiving Tim's letter that they had attended the funeral services for yet another

RESOLUTION

Marine from Saint Edward Parish, killed in action in South Vietnam. Lance Corporal Donald Frank Sansone, Hotel Company, Second Battalion, Fifth Marine Regiment of the First Marine Division, was killed in Quang Nam Province on November 6, 1967. A high school classmate, John McCartney, looked back: "I went to DePaul Academy with Don. He was my best friend on the football team. One time in practice we hit our heads together so hard that both of our helmets cracked. He was a great and funny guy." Another schoolmate, John Andres, Jr., remembered his friend Don, "I'll never forget all the great times we had in school, and the great times at the 'Y' dances. The last letter I received from him was only a few weeks before he was killed. He begged me not to go to Vietnam. I did go to the 'Nam, but I was lucky and made it back. As long as I live, I'll never forget him."

By the end of 1967, U.S. troop levels in Vietnam had reached 485,000. American casualty totals had climbed to 19,000 dead and 93,000 wounded, and the worst was still to come.

CHAPTER FOUR
DEVOTION

"An honorable people who lived up to their pledge to defend democracy, and did the best they could." It was February 28, 1968, and CBS News correspondent, Walter Cronkite, had just returned from Vietnam to give an analysis of what he had seen there. Cronkite had gone to Vietnam in the midst of the Tet Offensive, a military campaign by the forces of North Vietnam against American and South Vietnamese forces, to interview soldiers and civilians. Upon returning to the United States, Cronkite shared his observations with the American public. The newsman believed that although our country had given its very best effort in Vietnam, that in the final analysis, it was not going to be enough to achieve our objectives. Cronkite rejected President Lyndon Johnson's optimism for further military deployments to end the standoff between U.S. and Viet Cong forces. After hearing Cronkite's assessment, President Johnson was reported to have said, "If I've lost Cronkite, then I've lost Middle America."

Tim Fitzmaurice's paperwork had been processed. Prior to heading overseas, he was allowed a 15-day leave to head home to Chicago to spend time with his family before leaving for Vietnam. "The feelings during those days were mixed." Tim's sister, Ellen, recalled. "We were so happy to have Tim home again, but, at the same time, there was this somber mood. Grandma and Grandpa and Mom and Dad watched the news every night. We could all see the images of the war, and read about it in the papers. We knew about the guys from the neighborhood who had already been killed over there. Then came the end of January and things got even worse. Remember, Tim was home during the start of the Tet Offensive."

The Tet Offensive was the turning point for so many in the battle being waged at home for public support for the American war effort. Previously, the country was being told that the war in Vietnam was moving in the right direction and that the military was winning over the hearts and minds of the South Vietnamese people. The Tet Offensive was the largest military operation conducted by either side up to that point in the war. The initial attacks stunned the United States and South Vietnamese forces, but counter attacks contained and beat back the communist troops and inflicted massive casualties on them. Although the offensive was a military defeat for the communists, it had a profound effect on the U.S. government, and shocked the American public. "The feeling in our house was very different after Tet began," said Ellen. "The news was all bad and we were all so worried."

Tim Fitzmaurice reconnected with his friend, Bryan Dillon, while he was home. "It was great to see him," Bryan remembered. "We decided that before Tim shipped out, the two of us would go to a local recruiter to get me signed up for the Marines. They had something called the 'buddy plan' back then. If a current Marine could get a friend of his to sign up, then that Marine would get an extra five days added on to any leave. The only problem was that Tim knew that there was a two-year enlistment available, but the first two recruiters that we went to wouldn't allow me to have the two-year deal. They wouldn't give me anything less than a three-year option. Tim said he was positive that there was a two-year plan available, and, sure enough, the third recruiter that we hit OK'd my two-year enlistment. So that's how Tim was able to stretch his fifteen day leave into a twenty day leave before he left."

Bryan Dillon did not want to wait and take his chances with the draft. If he was going to serve his country, it was going to be with the Marine Corps. "It was just the way it was back then. There was this feeling of inevitability hanging over all of us at the time. You were going -- you might as well have a little control over the situation. My grandfather, my namesake, was a Marine in World War I. I don't know if I was necessarily, or consciously, trying to follow in his footsteps, but we did think that this was our war, our turn. Our Dads were in World War II, and now it was our time. Still, I was watching the news at night, and reading the papers, too. I could see what was waiting for all of us in Vietnam, and when the recruiter told me that I could wait for four months before having to start boot camp, I thought that might be a pretty good idea."

It was interesting to note that the feeling among Vietnam veterans that Vietnam was their war, and that this time it was their turn to go and do the fighting, was not a feeling that was unanimously shared by their World War II-era parents. Bryan's father, Bob Dillon, a United States Navy veteran of operations in the Pacific theatre during World War II, had witnessed the brutalities of war. Bob had been stationed on a destroyer escort ship, the *U.S.S. Elden*, which prowled the vast Pacific Ocean ahead of U.S. destroyer task forces, searching for Japanese submarines and trying to make safe the way for American naval battle groups. The *Elden* saw action in the harrowing campaign to drive the Japanese from the

Marianas Island chain. She patrolled off Tinian Island to prevent enemy troops from landing behind American lines on Saipan Island. After anti-submarine patrol off Eniwetok Atoll, the *Elden* returned to screening transports at Saipan, and delivering harassing fire on Tinian. "I remember seeing all those dead bodies floating in the water," Bob Dillon said, in recalling his duty off of Saipan. Rather than being taken captive by the advancing U.S. Marines, over 1,000 Japanese civilians committed suicide in the last days of the battle for Saipan, many jumping into the Pacific Ocean from a cliff at the northern tip of the island. Returning to the subject of his son's war, Bob added, "But we never should have been in Vietnam. We shouldn't have had to be the ones policing the world. We lost so many young guys."

Tim Fitzmaurice picked an interesting time to commit to Vietnam, as many of the architects and believers in our involvement in the war were beginning to plan their own personal withdrawals from the conflict. One day after Tim's November 28, 1967, letter to Cindy Koenig telling her of his decision to go to Vietnam, United States Defense Secretary Robert S. McNamara announced his intention to resign. The resignation had followed a memo that McNamara had sent to President Johnson recommending that Johnson freeze U.S. troop levels, stop bombing North Vietnam, and hand over the ground combat responsibilities completely to the South Vietnamese. It was a change of heart that infuriated President Johnson. After all, it was Secretary McNamara who had so personally engineered the U.S. initial involvement and troop buildup in Vietnam that the undertaking itself came to be known in some circles as "McNamara's War." McNamara was a Harvard-schooled business executive before being selected as President John F. Kennedy's Defense Secretary. One of the many Kennedy administration holdovers in the Johnson White House, McNamara brought a business-like approach to the Vietnam war's execution. Statistical analysis was to be the United States military's distinct advantage in taking the war to the Viet Cong and North Vietnamese. In McNamara's thinking, the numbers were all on the side of the U.S. From bombing sorties to body counts, there was no way that the enemy could withstand the sheer advantages that American forces could bring to the field with men and material. When the analysis did not bear fruit by way of ceasing enemy activity in South Vietnam, McNamara came to the conclusion that the war could not be won in the way that had been envisioned, and expressed his doubts to President Johnson. Johnson could not abide the opinion of his Defense Secretary that the American effort in Vietnam would not result in victory. McNamara would be dispatched to become the head of the World Bank. In a tearful goodbye ceremony at the White House on February 29, 1968, with U.S. troops in the field and the Tet Offensive still raging, McNamara withdrew himself from Vietnam.

For President Johnson, however, it was the defection of Walter Cronkite from the list of believers in victory in Vietnam that was the greater blow. It was two nights before Defense Secretary McNamara's White House farewell that Cronkite had opined at the end of his nightly news broadcast that the best we could say after three years of brutal fighting was that we were "mired in stalemate" and it was time for a negotiated exit from Vietnam. This time it was not a senior administration official who was delivering sobering news to Johnson, it was Cronkite. Johnson is said to have spoken of Cronkite as the voice of Middle America, and Johnson began to seriously worry that he had lost his broad base of public support after Cronkite's televised editorial.

Yet another perceived casualty of the Tet Offensive was General William Westmoreland, commander of the American military forces in Vietnam. Although the decision for Westmoreland to step down had been made in late 1967, Westmoreland's leaving was widely seen in the media as punishment for being caught off-guard by the communist assaults in early 1968. On April 28, 1967, in an address to a joint session of Congress, General Westmoreland had spoken of the keys to American victory in Vietnam: "Backed at home by resolve, confidence, patience, determination, and continued support, we will prevail in Vietnam over the Communist aggression." It would be analyzed that Westmoreland's consistently upbeat assessments of the military situation in Vietnam made the ensuing shock at the onset of the Tet Offensive that much more severe. Westmoreland was relieved by General Creighton W. Abrams, with the official date of the change in commanders taking place on June 10, 1968.

Back at the Fitzmaurice home on Kewanee Avenue, Tim was hard at work taking advantage of the extra five days of leave he received for signing up Bryan Dillon. "It was so great having Tim at home," Tim's sister, Ellen, recalled. "The house was filled with the sound of his laughter and singing. Dad was very ill at that time, and it was impossible for him to do some of the work around the house that needed to get done. One of the things that Mom wanted taken care of was to get the front bedroom painted. I remember that Tim was painting the room green, and all the while singing the song by the New Christy Minstrels that went, 'green, green, it's green they say on the far side of the hill' -- very loudly. He also loved to tell stories. We used to call them 'Timmy Tales.' He would combine all the John Wayne movies that he had ever seen into hilarious stories. He would tell them to friends and family. His wit was a joy for everybody. His sense of humor filled every room in the house with laughter."

As the day of Tim's departure grew closer, the atmosphere turned solemn around the Fitzmaurice home. Sadness and worry were apparent, but those emotions were overwhelmed by stoicism and resignation. The country had called on Tim and he was going to Vietnam to answer that call. Grandma and Grandpa were indebted to their adopted country and service was the price one paid for that indebtedness. Tim's father, Michael, was resolutely patriotic and a fierce defender of America's role in the world. Ellen Fitzmaurice Shea recalled a conversation that she had overheard between her father and her brother, Tim, shortly before Tim's departure. "He told Dad that he *had* to go to Vietnam. What would he say to his own children if he didn't go?

My Dad nodded his head in affirmation and silence. Dad really understood Timmy's position." Tim's mother, Lubitza, put her faith in God that everything would turn out all right.

Tim Fitzmaurice was in the process of saying his goodbyes. He nervously joked with his friends that their turns would come. He talked with Bryan Dillon about the possibility of even meeting in Vietnam, once Bryan had finished with his initial training. He made arrangements with another good friend, Danny Boyle, to give him the ride to the airport for the first leg of his journey to Vietnam. Tim wanted Danny to drop him off because Tim felt that a family farewell at the airport would have been much too emotional.

On the morning that Tim left for Vietnam, the Fitzmaurice's treated themselves to donuts from a favorite nearby bakery called Weber's. There were hugs and tears as Grandma, Grandpa, Ellen, Jack, and Maureen wished Tim good luck, and tried to convince themselves that they would all see him again soon. Tim then turned to Michael, and father and son stoically and resolutely shook hands, staring at each other in mournful silence. When Tim came to bid his mother farewell, Lubitza placed a Rosary and a Miraculous Medal into Tim's hand. The Miraculous Medal was carried by Catholics who believed that if worn with faith and devotion, the Medal would bring them special graces through the intercession of the Blessed Virgin Mary at the hour of death. Her eyes swollen with tears, Lubitza could barely speak as she gazed at the face of a son whom she loved more than herself. She took Tim into her arms for the last time, and silently asked God to watch over him. She kissed him goodbye, and as Tim headed to the door he turned back to take a final look at a family who would never see him again.

SMILE ON YOUR BROTHER

Timothy Fitzmaurice and his sisters, Maureen (L) and Ellen pictured on the morning Tim left home for Vietnam.

Tim had already been through an equally emotional goodbye the night before. He had gone to see his girlfriend, Cindy, one last time before leaving for Vietnam. They held hands and talked of the future. They loved each other and they would get through this together. Tim had let the military know that Cindy was his sister -- the designation of "sister" being necessary because, should the unthinkable occur, Tim knew that the military would only send informational telegrams to immediate family. There was time for one final embrace and as Tim looked into Cindy's eyes he whispered, "When I get back, I'll never leave you again."

CHAPTER FIVE
APPREHENSION

"Well, Goddamn, I finally made it! I was sure I'd be stationed in the Danang area, but right now I'm in Phu Bai, and it's hot here. They gave me a unit after I got here, Mike Company, Third Battalion, Fifth Marines. The company is in the bush right now and I'll be joining them in four or five days."

Those were the opening lines in Tim Fitzmaurice's first letter home to Cindy after his arrival in the Republic of Vietnam. Tim's inbound plane had landed on the tarmac at Danang Air Base in Quang Nam Province, and he disembarked with the other newly arrived Marines. Bryan Dillon vividly recalled his own landing at Danang Air Base: "I remember what it was like just getting off the plane there -- the smell and the incredible heat. I remember how scared I was. I was passing by Marines who had obviously been in country awhile. It was an image I'll never forget. There was a scene in a movie that captured that moment pretty well -- just the look they gave me scared me. Their faces weren't angry or sad, and it wasn't an exhausted look either. It's just like they were, I don't know... gone. It's hard to describe, but when I saw the look in their eyes, I knew I'd entered a different world."

Tim Fitzmaurice had to have had some of the same thoughts as Bryan Dillon later did. The fear, the dread, the "what have I gotten myself into" feeling. It was a disconsolate sensation of realizing that he could have simply served out the remainder of his enlistment in the relative safety of Guantanamo Bay. He didn't have to be here, but there wasn't time to think about that now. The "boots," as the newly-arrived Marines were called, were quickly hustled to a processing area and handed their orders to a dispersing officer. After a short wait, Tim and a group of Marines were herded on to a helicopter for the ride to Phu Bai Combat Base. At Phu Bai, Tim spent his first few days getting an indoctrination into life as a combat Marine in Vietnam. His days were filled with updates on the situation in the field, getting the supplies needed for life in the bush, and instructions on what to expect during combat operations. Tim was scheduled to join his unit, Mike Company, Third Battalion, Fifth Marines (Mike 3/5), on March 31, 1968.

Back home, another important event was taking place on March 31, 1968. Just as Tim

Fitzmaurice had joined his unit in the field, President Lyndon B. Johnson gave a speech to the nation announcing, in effect, his own personal exodus from Vietnam. With his Defense Secretary, Robert McNamara, and his Commanding General, William Westmoreland, departing, and with the "voice of Middle America," Walter Cronkite, coming out against the prosecution of the war, President Johnson began to re-think his approach to the conflict in Vietnam. Public opinion about the war had turned decidedly negative after the Tet Offensive, and a strong, charismatic candidate had emerged to challenge Johnson for the Democratic nomination for President. New York Senator Robert F. Kennedy was gaining support with his anti-war political agenda, and was seen as the major threat to a second term for the Johnson administration. It was in light of all of these new developments, which had overwhelmed the Johnson White House in a matter of just a few months, that the President took to the air waves to address a national television audience on March 31, 1968. With the battle for the Marine Corps outpost at Khe Sanh, the largest battle of the Tet Offensive, still in doubt, Johnson opened his speech with talk of peace in Vietnam. Because of political expediency, and the facts on the ground in Vietnam, Johnson expectedly announced a change in military strategy. But it was the content at the end of his speech that shocked the nation, "With American sons in the fields far away, with America's future under challenge right here at home, with our hopes, and the world's hopes for peace in the balance every day, I do not believe that I should devote an hour or a day of my time to any personal partisan causes, or to any duties other than the awesome duties of this office -- the presidency of your country. Accordingly, I shall not seek, and I will not accept, the nomination of my party for another term as your president." Lyndon Johnson had begun his own withdrawal from Vietnam, just as Lance Corporal Timothy Fitzmaurice was joining the war.

"Why's everybody going to the Fifth Marines? They can't need that many replacements, can they?" That was the initial reaction of Private First Class Johnnie Clark, in his book *Guns Up -- The Story of a Marine Rifle Company in Vietnam,* as Clark received his own assignment to the Fifth Marine Regiment. Tim Fitzmaurice may have been asking himself the same question when he found out about his new unit during his introduction to Vietnam at Phu Bai Combat Base. Phu Bai was the headquarters of the Fifth Marine Regiment, and as described by PFC Johnnie Clark, "a filthy, dust-covered tent city, but paradise compared to the bush." Tim's unit had been decimated by almost continuous combat since the start of the Tet Offensive, sustaining massive casualties in campaigns to liberate Danang and Hue City. The need for replacements was, unfortunately, constant.

Tim Fitzmaurice may not have known it at the time, but the Fifth Marine Regiment had a long and storied history in the annals of the Marine Corps. Activated on June 8, 1917, at the Philadelphia Navy Yard, they immediately set sail for France to take part in World War I. After encountering brutal combat for over a year, the Fifth Marine Regiment would be involved in one of the most legendary engagements in Marine Corps history. Belleau Wood became a seminal battle in the lore of the Corps. It was at Belleau Wood where Marine Captain Lloyd W. Williams said to his Marines who were repeatedly told to turn back by retreating French forces in the face of a German onslaught, "Retreat? Hell, we just got here!" It was at Belleau Wood where Marine Gunnery Sergeant Dan Daly, a recipient of two Congressional Medals of Honor, urged his company forward into the attack with the immortal words, "Come on you sons of bitches, do you want to live forever?" It was also at Belleau Wood where the Germans gave the Marines one of their most cherished nicknames, *"Teufelshunde"*, Devil Dogs. Most famous, however, were the words of General Black Jack Pershing, commander of the Allied Expeditionary Force during World War I, when he exclaimed after the battle at Belleau Wood, "The deadliest weapon in the world is a Marine and his rifle."

After World War I, the next chance that the Fifth Marine Regiment would get to distinguish themselves would be the bloody, island-hopping campaigns of World War II. Places that will live on forever in the history of American military heroism -- Guadalcanal, New Britain, Peleliu, Okinawa -- became vicious, bloody killing fields for the men of the Fifth Marines.

The Fifth Marine Regiment was called upon again during the Korean War. Deploying to the Pusan Perimeter in August of 1950, the Fifth Marines participated in the historic Inchon Landing and the battle of the Chosin Reservoir. Commanding General Louis B. "Chesty" Puller etched his name into Marine Corps history at the Chosin Reservoir with his actions and quotes such as, "We're surrounded -- that simplifies the problem," and "Remember, you're Marines. All the Communists in hell can't overrun you."

Leaving Korea, after defending the Korean demilitarized zone until 1955, it would be eleven more years until the Fifth Marine Regiment would once again be thrust into harm's way.

The war of attrition being fought in Vietnam required a different kind of strategy than a conventional type of conflict, where land is fought for and the victor occupies the contested land, and then attempts to win more battles to drive the opposing forces from the territory in order to claim ultimate victory. In Vietnam, United States and South Vietnamese forces were fighting two separate enemies - the North Vietnamese Army (NVA), and the insurgent forces of the Vietcong (VC). Under the command of General William Westmoreland, the goal was for the U.S. and its South Vietnamese allies to engage the enemy forces where they could be found, and with the aid of the overwhelming military advantages of the American war arsenal, simply destroy more NVA and VC men and material than the enemy could absorb, thereby devastating their ability and their will to continue the fight. This strategy required greater and greater amounts of U.S. troops, however, as the war escalated. So, on March 5, 1966, the Fifth Marine Regiment was deployed to Vietnam. The Fifth Marines didn't waste any time getting into the thick of things, as they swept into action in operations in and around the Marine Corps bases at Chu Lai and Tam Ky, in the northernmost provinces of South Vietnam.

"You didn't want to get too friendly with the new guys, so many of them didn't last long," Lance Corporal Jerry Lomax recalled. "I joined Mike 3/5 in February of '68, about a month and a half before Tim got there. The guys had been fighting since the start of Tet. I had so many friends who were killed."

The Fifth Marine Regiment had spent the entire month of February, 1968, in the brutal house-to-house fighting to liberate the South Vietnamese city of Hue. It was one of the most famous battles of the Vietnam war which left the jewel of Southeast Asia, the Imperial City of Hue, in ruins. After the recapture of Hue, the Fifth Marine Regiment was sent down to Danang. Intelligence had reports that North Vietnamese Army forces would next attack there, and the Fifth Marines would be counted on as one of the units who were given the task of repelling the enemy assault. Tim Fitzmaurice joined his new outfit just as they had finished with the successful defense of Danang. The Fifth Marine Regiment was making preparations for a new mission named Operation Baxter Garden, which immediately threw Tim into the ferocity of combat. During the seven-day operation, the Fifth Marines, supported by two battalions of South Vietnamese soldiers, engaged enemy platoon-sized forces. Most of the Marine casualties, however, were the result of triggering enemy land mines. The Marines sustained 13 dead and 55 wounded.

"Baxter Garden took a lot out of me. One day I'll tell you all about it," Tim wrote his girlfriend, Cindy. "We lost a lot of men up there and didn't even get a crack at Charlie. I think that's about the hardest thing to take. All these booby traps are just for harassment and to demoralize the troops. It works too! I wish I could get rid of my radio, it sure gets heavy. One day I was walking across a rice paddy, knee-deep in water and mud, when I slipped and fell backwards. Normally with my radio and all my gear on it takes one man to help me on my feet when I'm on solid ground. This time it took three people to get me out before I drowned.

It was nearly all over for me because I don't swim too good with my radio on. You should have heard the language that passed over my virgin lips -- simply disgusting. By the way, rice paddy water tastes worse than it smells. It's hard to believe, but I'm one of the few people who could verify that fact. Anyhow, Operation Baxter Garden is over and I'm in Troui Village now, trying to keep Charlie from drafting the local yokels into the wrong army."

The initial phase of what came to be known as Operation Houston, and the next assignment, was a bridge security detail for Tim's Marines. The Troui River Bridge was a key link in the need to keep traffic and supplies moving up and down Highway One, the main South Vietnamese roadway. Just two weeks prior to Mike 3/5's new detail, the bridge had been overrun and destroyed by large elements of main force North Vietnamese Army and Vietcong units. The bridge was now being rebuilt by members of the United States Navy

Seabees. The Seabees needed protection as they went about their vital work of reconstructing this important supply line. Tim's days were filled with the mundane and arduous tasks of filling sand bags and fortifying bunkers. "We were all scared at Troui Bridge," Lance Corporal Jerry Lomax noted. "We always thought that another ambush was coming as soon as the bridge was operational again. We were an under strength company to begin with. We only had about 90 guys, compared to a normal strength company of around 200 men. Nighttime was the worst."

The Marines felt that they owned the daytime due to their overwhelming advantage in firepower. But it was at night when advantage switched to the Viet Cong (VC) and the North Vietnamese (NVA). Because of this, nights were spent patrolling the areas adjacent to the bridge, searching for enemy activity. The theory was that it was better for the Marines to go out to engage the enemy forces rather than sit back and wait for an attack that would come at the time and choosing of the VC and NVA. Nine-man Marine ambush teams would leave the relative security of the area around the bridge to look for signs of an impending attack. It wasn't long before Tim got his chance to take part in these dangerous patrols. He wrote his girlfriend, Cindy, of his pride in these missions, but wouldn't speak of the inherent dangers that accompanied them. "OK, important news! I am now a member of the First Platoon ambush team, and we're good! Everyone in the battalion knows about us and our Colonel call us 'The Professionals,' isn't that nifty! I'll bet you're real proud of me now. The VC blew two bridges this week on Highway One and we're supposed to be next. But I guess Charlie got the word that 'the kid' was here now because he didn't try it last night."

Filling sandbags and providing security for the Seabees by day, and taking part in nighttime ambushes was exhausting and dangerous work, but Tim was still being told by some of the "salts," Marines who had been in country for a long while, that bridge duty was a piece of cake compared to life in the bush. The bush was that vast expanse of area "out there," away from the towns and villages and the fortified bases. The bush was owned and operated by "Charlie" -- the NVA and VC -- and it was there where the enemy held all the advantage. The bush for Charlie was familiar terrain, with a compliant population in many cases, and the ability to pick and choose the time and place for each engagement to maximize the devastating effect.

It wasn't long before the Marines of Mike 3/5 were given a new set of orders. They left behind the Troui River bridge detail to another Marine Corps unit, and they headed out into the bush as part of a lead element in a second phase of Operation Houston, now renamed as Operation

Houston II. The assignment for Tim, and the men of Mike 3/5, was a security sweep of the area adjacent to Highway One. Highway One ran north and south like a coastal spine down the length of the country. It was the primary supply route for everything from commerce to military movements. It was vital to keep the route open and secure. Mike 3/5 moved out to an area south of Phu Bai combat base, near a region called the Hai Van Pass. The Hai Van Pass was rugged, mountainous terrain, which made for incredibly difficult and dangerous patrolling. The first stopping point was a small hamlet named Langco Village. Today's tourist literature calls the area an ideal place for beach lovers. "Langco Village is next to National Highway One and near the Hai Van Pass. Langco Beach, with its gradually sloping white sand leading down to the blue sea, is an attractive destination for both domestic and international tourists. The village takes its name from the French L'an Co meaning "Stork Village'".

Tim and the rest of the Marines of Mike 3/5 weren't finding the area to be as inviting as the current tourist literature makes it out to be. Tim wrote to Cindy: "We went on a patrol this morning and it was so hot I didn't think we'd ever get back. The only thing we're doing now is pulling patrols down Highway One from about 15 miles north of Danang to the Hai Van Pass, about 20 miles all together. We had a lot of guys fall out while on the operation between Langco and the Pass, but there isn't any excuse for it. The way I see it, it's a matter of personal pride. I think if a machine gunner can carry a bulky M-60 weighing 23 pounds then I can carry a 25 pound radio on my back. Sounds funny doesn't it? As long as one man keeps going, I can't see any reason why I can't too. I sure get tired of being dirty. I haven't had a shower or taken my boots off for over a week. But what can I say; they can't keep me here forever."

Back in Chicago, the overall feeling was one of worry and despair. Just over a week after Tim Fitzmaurice had arrived in Vietnam, Dr. Martin Luther King, Jr. was assassinated in Memphis, Tennessee, on April 4, 1968. The streets of Chicago exploded in rage, revolt, and destruction. Arson and looting were rampant, causing Chicago Mayor Richard J. Daley to impose a city-wide curfew. By April 6, more than 6,700 Illinois National Guard troops were brought in to quell the violence. President Johnson sent an additional 5,000 U.S. Army troops to Chicago. It was during this period that Mayor Daley issued his infamous "shoot to kill" order directed against suspected arsonists and looters. "It was such a tumultuous time," Tim's sister, Ellen, said. "There was rioting in the streets, and demonstrations in downtown Chicago and on some of the college campuses. And always there was the dreadful news coming from Vietnam on our TV every night. We were all so worried about

Tim, but we didn't really talk about it. My Dad was really sick, and Mom, I think, just put her faith in God that everything would be okay and Tim would make it through and come home."

There was something eerily ominous in the tone of the next letter that Cindy received from Tim. He seemed to have a premonition about the danger that awaited him in the upcoming phase of the operation. "Sorry I haven't written, but we just got some bad news last night. The company is going back up into the mountains. It's pretty bad up there, and I'm not too anxious to go. I really wish I were home now! I just don't like going back up there. But what the hell, it doesn't make any difference where I go, I'm pretty lucky at any rate. I hope I get enough time to write you. Living out here is definitely putting a malfunction in my schedule. I know Bryan would probably like it here, he's goofy that way. I dropped him a letter the last time I wrote to you and he's all excited about his trip to San Diego. He'll probably make it over here before too long. Well, I guess that's about it. Take care of yourself sweetheart, and don't worry about me, 'cause I'm going to be just fine."

CHAPTER SIX
DISSOLUTION

During the early morning hours of May 5, 1968, North Vietnamese and Vietcong units initiated Phase II of the Tet Offensive. These attacks became known as the May Offensive or "Little Tet." Communist forces had assaulted 119 targets throughout South Vietnam, including another thrust into South Vietnam's capital, Saigon. Repelling these attacks and beating back the enemy proved to be incredibly costly to American forces. The May Offensive would end up being much bloodier than the initial phases of the Tet Offensive, with over 5,100 American casualties including almost 1,200 killed.

On May 7, 1968, orders came down to Tim Fitzmaurice and the rest of Mike Company. They headed out from Langco Village and began an ascent of a very steep hill. On the Marine Corps intelligence map it was known as Hill 1192 -- so named because it was 1192 meters high. Tim's apprehension about the patrol was eased somewhat when word got passed back to the men that Marine reconnaissance had detected no signs of enemy activity in the area. The men were now being told that this was going to be just a stroll. "Leave the flak jackets and the heavy gear behind, they told us," Jerry Lomax recalled. "Recon showed no trouble, so we felt safe and secure. And let me tell you, we were happy to leave all of that heavy shit behind. It was really hot, and that hill was really steep. It was a pretty area though, and thank God there were some cold streams running through there, and some pools of water. We humped all day but didn't see any gooks. We settled in for the night and had to try and sleep with ponchos over our heads because the mosquitoes were so bad."

As Tim Fitzmaurice was heading up Hill 1192, his mother, Lubitza, was back at home trying to go on with her day-to-day activities. She wrote Tim on May 7, "We're all pretty good. Daddy caught a cold, which isn't good for him. But he's staying in bed and he'll be OK soon. Grandma has to rest more, too. Her heart is so bad. She wants to make more cookies for you -- she's so cute. Last night Denny and Ellen went down to see Grandpa and Grandma, and she starts pulling out all of the pictures of you kids. She and Grandpa are so proud of you. Denny enjoyed it. He's so nice. He was dressed in his Army dress blues for the military ball. Ellen had on a formal. Please take care of yourself. Please be careful. Keep your rifle clean so you don't run into trouble. Please write soon. We love you and miss you very much."

May 8, 1968, dawned early as the Marines of Mike 3/5 resumed their patrol up the steep slopes of Hill 1192. So far, so good, Tim had to have been thinking as the company was making its way to the top of the hill without any sign of the enemy. The conditions were hot and miserable, and climbing the torturous terrain was exhausting to the men, but as long as there continued to be an absence of Charlie, things could be much worse. After a few hours, the company was given the signal to stop for a rest. The Marines brought out their cigarettes to enjoy a smoke and talk about how glad they were that they didn't have to bring all of their extra supplies up the hill. The oppressive heat would surely have put a few guys out of commission if they were carrying their full complement of gear. Just as the order went down the line to "saddle up," some shots rang out, and then, just as quickly, things fell silent. While everyone scrambled for cover, the call came for "corpsman up". The men knew that someone had been hit. The shots had come from enemy snipers and two Marines were down. Dead was Private First Class Jack Fiffe from Albany, New York. Lance Corporal Dale Andrews from Pontiac, Michigan, was gravely wounded, and would later die. The sniper activity let Mike 3/5's company commander, Captain Frank Pacello, know that there was serious trouble up ahead. Skipper Pacello told his Gunnery Sergeant, Lawrence Harville, to send a four-man fire team ahead of the rest of the company on a recon mission to mark a trail. Lance Corporal Jerry Lomax was one of the recon team members. "We were sent to mark a trail up ahead and the first thing we saw were the hootches and a small group of gooks. I never thought they could be NVA, I thought they were friendlies. The Gunny caught up to us and sent for a machine gun team to help us go after the gooks. We charged the hootches and were able to blow up one of them with a LAWS (light anti-tank weapon) rocket that I carried. We got most of the guys who were around the hootches, but a couple got away through tunnels." The commanding officer and the rest of the company, including Tim Fitzmaurice, came up to join the recon team to form a protective perimeter to settle in for the night. The sniper fire continued, however, until darkness set in, with Tim and the rest of the Marines getting continually frustrated because they didn't know where the shots were coming from. Private First Class Richard Seng, age 19, from Allentown, Pennsylvania, fell victim to a sniper round and became the third member of Mike 3/5 to be killed in the escalating battle for Hill 1192. The night passed slowly inside the Marine perimeter. Tim could only wonder what the morning would bring, as the premonition that he had expressed to his girlfriend, Cindy, about this patrol was becoming horribly true.

DISSOLUTION

Lubitza Fitzmaurice was watching the news reports from Vietnam every night and devouring the newspapers for any information on the war, and specifically Tim's unit. The news was all bad and troubled her greatly. She found comfort in her now almost daily letters to her beloved son. May 9, 1968, would be no exception. "Dad went to the doctor today, all is the same. Bryan Dillon is coming over next week with his mother before he leaves for boot camp. Denny is going to Camp McCoy in Wisconsin for training. Ellen misses him when he goes to Wisconsin, so she'll have it bad when he goes away for two years. Cindy can cheer her up -- she knows. Sweet girl Cindy. We all like her very much. I go down to see her as often as I can. We hope you are OK and things are not too bad where you are. We worry about you and wish we could do something to make things easier for you. All we can really do is hope and pray that you'll be well and safe from injury. Please take care of yourself and please write soon. Grandma and Grandpa send their love. Love Mom and all."

The Marines of Mike Company moved out early on the morning of May 9, 1968. Their destination was to finally reach the top of the hill and begin to head down the other side. "Everybody was really on edge," Captain Frank Pacello remembered. "We'd lost three guys already and we were an under strength company to begin with. We started up that hill with only about 90 guys -- a regular company should have more than 200." Skipper Pacello sent out a scout team over the top of the hill to get an idea of what might lay up ahead. Corporal Jerry Lomax was chosen again to be part of that scout team. "We couldn't have been more than fifty yards over the top of that hill, and I simply could not believe what I saw. There were NVA all over the place, so I radioed back to Pacello that there's a shitload of gooks up here." Almost immediately, the NVA opened up on the Marines with small arms fire and machine guns. One of the scout team members, Private First Class Richard Huffman from Troutsville, Pennsylvania, who had been in Vietnam for less than a month, was quickly wounded. PFC Huffman would later die from his wounds, as the vastly outnumbered Marines tried in vain to get to the scout team position and rescue them. Lance Corporal Jim Blankenheim was a junior Forward Air Controller with Mike Company during the battle for Hill 1192. A Navy Commendation Medal recipient for his heroic actions on that savage hilltop, Blankenheim was responsible for maintaining the company's protective artillery and tactical air support during the entire battle. His memory of the initial phase of the battle was very vivid. "I remember as we reached the summit that we heard gunfire over the top. They told us that the point elements had made contact, and that we were fighting within a series of hootches. We all knew that hootches meant a base camp, but not until later did we find out just how big the base camp was." The Marine Corps official after-activity report described the ensuing battle in very stark terms. "Company Mike's combat patrol inadvertently happened upon an NVA base camp and was heavily engaged in extremely torturous terrain."

Captain Frank Pacello, Commanding Officer of Mike Company, Third Battalion, Fifth Marine Regiment.

Tim Fitzmaurice was back with the rest of the men when the word came down to the platoon commanders that the company would mount a full-out assault over the hill to come to the aid of the pinned-down scout team. Jerry Lomax emotionally recalled, "I watched as the whole company came charging over the top of the hill. It was one of the most incredible things that I have ever seen. It was like something out of the movies." After the assault, the entire company was now on the far side of the ridge, and it was determined that the Marines were up against a much larger force. Immediate air support was needed if they had any chance of survival. Air strikes were called against the enemy positions, but it quickly became clear that because of the extremely dense terrain air support was not going to be able to deliver the desired effectiveness on the enemy. The aircraft pilots simply couldn't distinguish between friendly and enemy forces through the impenetrable jungle canopy.

Mike Company was spread out in a small perimeter position and it was decided that if air support was not going to be an option, then artillery would have to be brought in to keep the North Vietnamese Army's overwhelming force from overrunning the Marines. The situation was very quickly becoming dire.

Senior Forward Air Controller, Corporal Dave Burnham, choked back tears recalling the courage of the Mike 3/5 Marines. "I couldn't believe the heroism of those grunts. They were surrounded and outmanned and they never stopped fighting. They were getting shot to pieces, but they'd still stick their heads up and keep fighting." Corporal Burnham would go on to receive the Navy Commendation Medal for his own courageous actions on Hill 1192. By coordinating artillery, air support, and medevac rescues, Burnham saved the lives of countless brother Marines.

DISSOLUTION

Dave Burnham (L) and Jim Blankenheim -- two of the heroes of the battle for Hill 1192. They are pictured in 2004 at a Mike 3/5 reunion, meeting again for the first time in 36 years.

As the battle wore on the casualties mounted for the Americans. Lance Corporal William Trent from East Peoria, Illinois, tried valiantly to rescue the pinned-down scout team. His posthumous

Navy Cross Citation read, "On May 9, 1968, when Company M encountered a large NVA force in Thua Thien Province, Corporal Trent's platoon came under heavy automatic weapons, and small arms fire. Reacting instantly, Corporal Trent, undaunted by the enemy fire that was erupting all around him, manned his machine gun and advanced against the enemy. Disregarding his own safety, he delivered effective fire into a fortified position, silencing the automatic weapon. Shifting his fire to another target of opportunity, he quickly annihilated a second enemy position. He then observed two NVA soldiers moving to occupy the first gun position. Instantly he seized his machine gun and a belt of ammunition and courageously advanced against the enemy-occupied position. Moving to within a few feet of the pinned-down enemy, he killed both hostile soldiers. Quickly emplacing his machine gun in the fortified position, he began firing into the enemy's flank. Although mortally wounded by an enemy hand grenade, he remained at his exposed position until elements of his platoon were able to maneuver forward." Private First Class Sam Cole, Jr. from San Francisco, California, who was part of the machine gun team with Corporal Trent, was also killed in the initial assault over the ridgeline.

Captain Pacello lamented the way things were done in Vietnam. "These kids were under fire right away. Because we were taking so many casualties, going on one operation after another, there was no chance for any unit cohesion. We were constantly trying to absorb new replacements. Some of these kids were on two-year enlistments. All they knew was boot camp, some advanced training, and then on to Vietnam, where they were thrown into almost continuous combat." Only six weeks into his tour, and Tim Fitzmaurice was in the middle of a battle that his commanding officer would describe as "Custer's Last Stand" -- fighting that was eyeball to eyeball.

The battle was raging for hours and dead and wounded Marines were all over the crest of the hill. Calls to the corpsmen for medical aid were constant. One of the people answering those calls was United States Navy Corpsman Third Class Harry "Doc" Bowman from Woodridge, New Jersey. The astounding heroism of "Doc" Bowman saved many lives on Hill 1192. On too many occasions, however, his was the last face a dying Marine would see on that horrible May 9. His selfless acts of bravery would eventually cost him his life. His loss devastated an entire company of Marines who were now battling for their very survival. Doc Bowman's Silver Star Citation read: "On May 9, 1968, HM3 Bowman's unit came under fire from a well-entrenched force wounding several Marines. Observing three injured Marines lying in an open area exposed to hostile fire, he courageously maneuvered across the fire swept terrain and carried the most seriously injured man to a position of safety. Returning to the hazardous area, he moved the second wounded Marine to a position of relative safety, and before reaching the remaining casualty, was wounded. Despite his injuries, he steadfastly continued toward his fallen comrade and was mortally wounded by heavy enemy fire." Corporal Rocco "Rock" Giambrocco remembered Doc Bowman's last minutes. "I saw Doc go out after a couple of guys and drag them in wounded. Then I saw him get hit. Then he got to a Marine and began working on him and he got hit again. He asked for cover and one guy went out to get him - I think Lomax, but I can't remember for sure. One time an automatic burst went in their direction and they shielded the body that Doc was working on. Then there was another burst and Doc caught a few in his side. He slumped over and died. I was crushed. I never thought Doc would get it."

Another Mike 3/5 Navy Corpsman would fall while administering aid to his downed comrades.

Charles "Doc" Mariskanish from Barnesboro, Pennsylvania merited his Silver Star by saving the lives of two Marines. His posthumous citation read: "Petty Officer Mariskanish's unit came under intense automatic weapons and small arms fire from a well-entrenched force of North Vietnamese Army Regulars, wounding three Marines who fell in an open area. Repeated attempts to evacuate the casualties failed due to the volume of heave enemy automatic weapons fire. Requesting his platoon to deliver covering fire, Petty Officer Mariskanish fearlessly crawled across the fire swept terrain on two separate occasions to evacuate the wounded Marines. As he attempted to reach the remaining casualty, Petty Officer Mariskanish was mortally wounded by the hostile fire. He gallantly gave his life in the service of his country."

The situation was becoming desperate and the Marines were in danger of becoming completely overrun and wiped out. Private First Class Fernando Alegria, who would receive the Bronze Star Medal for his actions on Hill 1192, was a radio operator with third platoon. He was next to Captain Pacello when he heard the Skipper telling his Colonel that the Marines were going to begin a withdrawal from the hill. The Colonel radioed back, "Negative Captain, you will stand your position and fight, and we will send up some relief."

In some areas of the battlefield the fighting was now hand-to-hand, with dead Marines found fallen right next to their North Vietnamese counterparts. Four more Marines would perish that May 9, 1968 on the murderous hell of Hill 1192. Lance Corporal Ronald Merkel from Waldron, Michigan, Private First Class Randolph Sterns from Tuscaloosa, Alabama, Private First Class Michael Micunek, from Detroit, Michigan, and the last Marine to die that day, a 20-year old Lance

Corporal from Kewanee Avenue and St. Edward Parish in Chicago. Timothy Fitzmaurice was so far from home.

CHAPTER SEVEN
DISTINCTION

"When I get back, I'll never leave you again." Those were the words that Tim Fitzmaurice left with Cindy Koenig before leaving for Vietnam. "He just didn't want anyone to think that he was avoiding his duty. But I could start to tell by his letters that some regret about his decision was beginning to show," Cindy reflected. Tim wrote her, "One of these days I'll have to figure out how long I have to do here yet in the Corps.

I'm about ready to come home now." Each succeeding letter from Tim to Cindy was filled with a longing for the war to be over and wishing for home. "I heard the President's speech the other day. Maybe he'll end the war so I can go home. I've seen enough of the world sweetheart. I think I'm ready to come home to you now."

By now every man in Mike Company, Third Battalion, Fifth Marine Regiment knew that the unit was in danger of being completely annihilated. Captain Frank Pacello described just what Mike 3/5 was facing. "It was a North Vietnamese Army city overlooking Danang. There were six 100-man mess halls, elaborate tunnel systems, huge weapons caches, and sizeable food stores. We were very fortunate to have come up the backside of the hill. In essence, we came in through the back door of their camp, and so we were somewhat of a surprise to them. Even though we were heavily outnumbered, the enemy never completely gained the initiative. But the sheer size of their force meant that we had to rely on artillery and air power if we had any chance of surviving. To keep from being overrun and slaughtered, we had to bring the incoming ordnance on top of our position. It was our only hope of survival because we were fighting nose-to-nose with the enemy." The thick jungle tree growth rendered air support futile, so the Marines turned to artillery support from Battery F, Second Battalion of the Eleventh Marine Regiment.

Near the end of the day's fighting on May 9, 1968, the Marines had to try to consolidate their remaining positions to create some type of defensive perimeter in order to try to last until the next morning. The incoming artillery shells were exploding all around them, as they tried to keep the advancing enemy from tearing into their defensive lines. Jerry Lomax remembered what happened next. "I recall it very vividly, Tim was accidentally killed by an artillery round that got too close. It was inevitable that somebody might get it, because Mike Company was in such deep shit that the artillery had to be close to everyone if we were going to make it. I was able to talk to Tim before he died. I told him that if we ever get out of this, we'll go straight to Chicago after our tour is over and get the biggest steak we could find. And then he died."

Timothy George Fitzmaurice, first-born son of Michael and Lubitza Fitzmaurice, grandson of Anna and Ilija Soraich, brother to Ellen, Jack, and Maureen Fitzmaurice, died on a blood-soaked hilltop in Thua Thien Province, South Vietnam on May 9, 1968.

DISTINCTION

Corporal Jerry Lomax of Mike Company, Third Battalion, Fifth Marine Regiment. Lomax offered words of comfort to a dying Timothy Fitzmaurice as the battle for Hill 1192 raged.

Back home in Chicago, Maureen Fitzmaurice was being awakened very early in the morning. "There was a presence in my room with me. Someone had touched me on my left shoulder. I sensed the touch as a warm, comforting, and reassuring feeling that spread through me. It was just beginning to get light outside, and as the last remnants of sleep began to clear, I realized that I was completely alone. I lay in bed for a long while, listening to my parents talking and drinking coffee in the kitchen. I got up, left my room, and stood before my parents. They immediately asked me what was wrong. 'Someone just touched my shoulder, I said.' I remember that they just turned and looked at each other for a long time without saying a word. Then they both gave me a hug and sent me back to bed."

There was no time for any of the surviving Marines of Mike Company to mourn their fallen comrades. May 10, 1968, brought another brutal day of fighting. The dead and wounded were multiplying rapidly, and the Marines were dangerously low on food, water, and ammunition to continue the fight for their survival. There was no way to bring in a medevac helicopter, or a re-supply chopper to the extremely remote area without creating some type of landing zone that would accommodate a helicopter. Captain Frank Pacello realized that they had to carve out an open space if they had any hope at all of getting off that hill. The Skipper had the men wrap C-4 plastic explosives around trees and then wrap all of that with detonation cord. The resulting explosion was incredible, as huge sections of trees were instantly cleared away. They called in the first chopper to evacuate the wounded. Lance Corporal Jim Blankenheim tells what happened next. "We were able to load 16 wounded on that first chopper when it started to lift up. Suddenly I noticed it was backing down the ridge toward the jungle canopy. I called the pilot and told him to stop going back or he was going to hit the trees. He kept going back more and more. Now I'm screaming, 'you're going to hit the trees,' and he's calling back that he's losing his cushion and can't hold it. The next thing

I know his chopper blades are flying through the trees above my head, and the chopper flips on its side and crashes. Wounded Marines are scattered everywhere and the chopper is leaking flight fuel and could ignite at any second. The other Marines never hesitated for an instant -- they ran to the aid of their wounded buddies and pulled them away from the area around the downed chopper." Luckily for the Marines, the damaged helicopter did not explode and a second medevac helicopter was called in to extricate the wounded Leathernecks. Captain Pacello recalled, "The amount of fire that these medevac choppers took coming in to get our wounded was immense. I don't know how they made it out of there without getting shot down. Those pilots were incredible heroes."

The decision was made not to put helicopter crews at risk removing the dead from the battlefield in the middle of an ongoing fight.

The dead Marines were stacked in the rear of the fighting area to keep away from the enemy. Those Marines had to wait for the end of the battle before they could leave the hill. The situation was still dire as the heavily outnumbered Marines fought for two more days until elements of India Company, Second Battalion of the Fifth Marine Regiment fought their way to the top of Hill 1192 to assist Mike Company in driving the North Vietnamese off of their positions and the abandonment of their base camp. The helicopters were then called in to remove the Marine dead from the battlefield.

Mike 3/5 Marines, Corporal Jim Quinn and senior Forward Air Controller Corporal Dave Burnham, were two of the Marines who were given the unenviable task of putting their deceased brothers into body bags to prepare them to be loaded on to the choppers. Burnham remembered, "I got into it with some Sergeant from India Company, who made a wisecrack about how they had to come up here and save our asses. He must not have liked my response, because he ordered me to help out on the body bag detail. You have to remember, these bodies had been piled up in the rear, some of them for as many as five days in 105-degree heat and humidity. The condition of those bodies, and putting them into those bags, is something that will stay with me forever. I came home from Vietnam, and spent the better part of thirty years numbing myself with drugs and alcohol trying to remove those images from my mind. I would think about that for hours every day. I kept those feelings inside and never talked about it. I finally realized that the alcohol and drugs were only a crutch I used to try to forget. I began to go to reunions, to hook up with my old Marine buddies. It was better to talk about it than to try to keep everything bottled up inside. Also, try to think what it was like for us knowing for five days and nights that we were outnumbered about 600 NVA to 90 of us. We really thought we were going to be overrun. I think we all must have psychological damage from that. So much of it could have been avoided, though. Pacello wanted to pull back on the second day, but the Colonel told him to hold his position -- what an asshole!"

Jim Quinn was a city kid from the southside of Chicago. He was born and raised in Saint Clotilde Parish at 84th Street and South Calumet Avenue. A rapidly disintegrating neighborhood, however, prompted Jim's family to move to Chicago's northside parish of Queen of All Saints. Jim graduated from Loyola Academy High School in 1962 and then went on to study at Loyola University, graduating in 1966. After college he volunteered for the Marine Corps. "I had feelings of this being my turn. There wasn't even a thought of not serving. I wanted the Marines and I wanted an infantry unit in Vietnam. I was similar to Tim Fitzmaurice in that, initially, I was in a duty assignment that looked like I would not be sent to Vietnam, so I had to 'request mast' as they called it, which meant I had to ask for assignment to Vietnam."

Quinn arrived in Vietnam in early 1968 and served with Mike 3/5 until June. "When you're in fighting like what we experienced up on Hill 1192, you realize just how much fate is a factor on whether or not you make it out alive. None of those who died did anything wrong. You come out of situations like that with immense feelings of guilt. Why did I make it and they didn't? All the various 'what ifs' go through your mind. Hill 1192 was the worst combat that I saw during my entire tour, and I was on some pretty bad operations -- Allenbrook, Mameluke Thrust -- but Operation Houston was the worst by far. We were lucky to have Pacello as our Skipper. He was gung-ho, and we didn't always see eye-to-eye on things, but he saved lives, and the welfare of his men was always his top priority." Frank Pacello returned the compliment when he said of Quinn: "He was your typical Irishman. When he wasn't busy causing trouble, he was busy being a hero." True to Captain Pacello's description, Corporal Quinn distinguished himself on Hill 1192, receiving the Bronze Star Medal for his actions. His Citation read in part: "Disregarding his own safety, Corporal Quinn fearlessly maneuvered across the fire-swept terrain to the downed Marines' location, simultaneously delivering a heavy volume of fire upon the enemy emplacements. Reaching one of the wounded, he ignored the hostile fire impacting near him, and rapidly assisted the injured man to a position of relative safety. On two additional occasions, he unhesitatingly returned across the hazardously exposed area in order to move two additional casualties to covered positions. His heroic and timely actions inspired all those who observed him and were instrumental in saving the lives of three wounded comrades." But it was Quinn's final heroic action before leaving Hill 1192 that haunts him to this day. It was Jim Quinn who placed the corpse of Timothy Fitzmaurice into the body bag and zipped it closed. "I remember the Jolly Green Giant chopper coming in right before we left 1192. It came for the dead. The helicopter lowered a big net, and we loaded it up with body bags. How many dead? I remember 15-20. The dead had been laying there, stacked in a log pile, some for as many as five days in that jungle heat. That was a horrible experience and I remember after it was all over, going off by myself and beginning to write a letter home -- my letters never mentioned combat or casualties -- and I began to cry, to really weep, and I couldn't stop for over half an hour. It was tough to recover from 1192. We lost so many dead and wounded."

DISTINCTION

Corporal Jim Quinn of Mike Company, Third Battalion, Fifth Marine Regiment. Quinn would be called upon to place the corpse of Timothy Fitzmaurice into a body bag after the battle of Hill 1192.

CHAPTER EIGHT
DEVASTATION

"And then one Tuesday we didn't get a letter. Tim had always written home every week, and we would always get the letter on Tuesdays," Tim's sister, Ellen, remembered. Tuesday, May 14, 1968, had come and gone, and this time the mailman hadn't left a letter with the latest news from Tim. Real worry began to grip the family home. Michael Fitzmaurice now talked openly to his children about the dreams that he was having. Dreams about the difficulties that his son,

Tim, was enduring. Dreams depicting just how bad things were for his son in Vietnam. "No one wanted to really discuss the possibility of something happening to Tim," Ellen said. "But when there was no letter from him that week, Jack and I talked to each other about the bad feelings that we were both having. In front of Mom we would always be positive, but there was no doubt that it was the elephant in the room."

A mother's intuition is a funny thing. It's a gut instinct, a feeling in her heart that her child might be in pain or in danger. Lubitza Fitzmaurice came to rely on that instinct over the many years of raising her family. Her intuition was her guiding compass, it had never let her down. She *knew* when her children were in trouble and needed her. Lance Corporal Curtis Batten, who fought with the Marines of Mike 3/5 on Hill 1192, also knew the power of a mother's intuition. "On the morning of May 12, 1968, my mom and stepdad were in their kitchen eating breakfast. They were watching a morning news story about a Marine unit being pinned down and surrounded -- very vague. Mom just looked at my stepdad and said, 'that is Curt who they are talking about' -- something only a mother could understand. The really strange thing was that it happened on Mother's Day. We were on Hill 1192 for Mother's Day."

This time, however, Lubitza did not want to listen to what her heart was telling her. She would not allow herself to believe the worst about Tim. The thought of something happening to her child was too much to bear. She was going to reason with herself -- *Tim was alright, he just must have been too busy to write this week*. Lubitza then found solace where she always had when worry overcame her -- she wrote to Tim. On May 15, 1968, six days after her son had been killed, Lubitza picked up her pen and paper to talk to Tim one last time. "Dear Tim, last night Mrs. Dillon and Bryan came over. Bryan leaves for Camp Pendleton tomorrow morning. Cindy came over to say goodbye to him, too. We had a really nice visit. Bryan starts his boot training right away. I saw Cindy at work and invited her over. She is so sweet. What did everyone talk about? You, of course! They really do think that you are OK. We had a lot of fun, and we were glad that Bryan came over to wish him luck. We hope you are OK. We haven't had a letter from you in awhile, and you know how much we worry about you. We know things are hard for you. Please be careful and take care of yourself. Write soon. We all send our love."

The doorbell rang early on Thursday morning, May 16, 1968, at the Fitzmaurice home. It was 6 AM, but Michael was already awake. He was always up very early sitting in his favorite chair. He was spending a lot of time in that chair because sitting up was the only way he could partially relieve his labored breathing. On oxygen, and in the advanced stages of emphysema, Michael wasn't able to stray too far from his chair. Lubitza, too, was up early, preparing breakfast for her husband and for her daughter, Ellen, who was busy typing lesson plans for her student teaching sessions that she had scheduled for the day. Despite a busy morning household, visitors at this time of day were certainly a rarity. Ellen got up to answer the doorbell. "The first thing I saw was the Marine Corps car through the window and my heart sank. I opened the door to see a Marine standing there in his Class A uniform. He announced himself as Lieutenant Dial and asked to speak to my father. I pointed him over to Dad's chair." The Marine turned sharply and headed over to where Michael Fitzmaurice was seated. He stared at Michael for a brief moment before taking a deep breath to deliver the words, "On behalf of the Commandant of the Marine Corps, I deeply regret to inform you that your son has been killed in combat operations in the Republic of South Vietnam."

The words seemed to hang in the air for an eternity, as Michael turned and gazed at his wife, the silence only broken when Lubitza began to weep bitterly at the loss of her son. When Ellen began to cry the rest of the house awoke. "Timmy was killed," Ellen sobbed to Jack as he came into the living room. The words stopped Jack and he fell to the floor. He had fainted upon hearing that his brother was dead. Ten-year-old Maureen came out from her room to see her family in complete despair, and began to cry as well when told that her big brother was gone from her life. Jack was able to gather himself long enough to crawl back to his bed to dissolve in tears. Grandma and Grandpa had heard the commotion upstairs and opened their door to see the Marine Corps vehicle parked in front of the house. At the same time, their daughter, Lubitza, was collapsing down the stairs to tell them that her Timmy was gone. "You had to know Grandpa, Ellen recalled. He was a very gregarious and demonstrative man. When he heard that Timmy had been killed, he let out a cry that our neighbors would have had to have heard. When I saw him in that much pain, I began to cry even harder. Lieutenant Dial offered to go and help Grandma and Grandpa deal with their grief after he had listened to Grandpa's loud cry."

Although chaos reigned all around him, Lieutenant Dial stood steadfast in his resolve to inform Michael and Lubitza about the coming arrangements to get their son's body back to Chicago, and ready for burial. Ellen Fitzmaurice held her young sister, Maureen, closely to her, rigid, listening while the Marine continued his anguished duty. Maureen Fitzmaurice's childhood was dissolving with every word uttered by the young Marine officer. "Lieutenant Dial took very good care of our family," Ellen said. "He previewed the details of the funeral service; he gave us his home phone number; he warned us that a telegram would be arriving shortly confirming Timmy's death. I remember my Dad saying that he hoped that this was all a big mistake -- until that telegram arrived later in the day." The family's devastation only deepened when they were informed that Tim had been dead for a week. How could this have been? Why hadn't they been notified earlier? Lieutenant Dial informed them that because of the nature of the combat situation that Tim was involved in, it was impossible at that time to get accurate confirmation on the names of the dead and wounded. Compounding the family's agony was the fact that Tim's body would not be able to make it back to them for another week. Lieutenant Dial stayed with the family for a few additional hours explaining the specifics of the death protocol. The Fitzmaurice's were to be assigned a Marine Corps casualty escort who was to remain with Tim's body from the time he landed back in the United States until the time of his burial. When all of the family's questions had been answered, Ellen escorted Lieutenant Dial to the door. "When I opened the door I looked outside to see that the whole block was flying the American Flag. Kewanee Avenue was beautiful! I found out later that one of our neighbors had seen Lieutenant Dial at the base of our stairs before he entered our house. The Marine was stopping to collect himself before beginning his terrible duty. Our one neighbor saw this and spread the word to the rest of the block that something must have happened to Timmy."

Back inside the Fitzmaurice house, phone calls were now being made to let close friends and family know of the calamitous news. Ellen called her boyfriend, Dennis Shea, first to let him know about Tim. The news hit Dennis extremely hard -- not only for the grief brought on to the woman he loved, but mindful of the realities that he, too, would soon be facing.

Lubitza was the one who notified Tim's girlfriend, Cindy. "I was awakened by the call from Lubitza, and my reaction to the news of Tim's death has always troubled me. She told me that Tim had been killed and I screamed, 'you are lying, you are lying' and I hung up the phone and went back to bed. I hung up on her because, of course, I refused to believe that Tim was dead. I guess I never really thought that it was a possibility. I never did apologize to her for my reaction, but I think she understood."

Word about the death of Tim Fitzmaurice quickly got around to most of the friends and family, but there was one person who could not be reached; one person left who didn't know that Tim was gone. Bryan Dillon was flying out to Marine Corps boot camp recruit training in San Diego, California, on the morning of May 16, 1968. He had no idea of the heartbreaking tragedy that was unfolding at the exact same time at Tim's home. Bryan was setting his course, following in Tim's footsteps, on the way to Vietnam. Brand new Marine Corps recruits had their hands full as they began their boot camp training. The stress and the strain imposed on the recruits by callous and intimidating drill instructors during the initial indoctrination into Marine Corps life was enough to break many a young man. How and when was the right time to tell Bryan that his best friend was dead?

Bryan's father, Bob Dillon, had just returned from the Chicago airport after having dropped Bryan there for his flight to San Diego, when he received word that Tim Fitzmaurice had been killed. "Obviously the news of Tim's death was a huge shock to us," Bob Dillon recalled. "Bryan had just left for boot camp, and we had no idea what we should do or how we should tell him. It was suggested to us that we call a Marine Corps recruiter to ask for advice on how to handle this. The recruiter told us not to contact Bryan and burden him with this terrible news. The recruiter reminded us that Bryan was about to enter one of the most mentally and physically challenging periods of his life. He was going to need 100 percent focus on the tasks at hand or he would never be able to survive boot training. Telling Bryan that Tim was dead was going to have to be postponed, but we didn't know if there was ever going to be a good time to do it."

In the end, it wasn't either of Bryan Dillon's parents who ended up breaking the news. "I had been at boot camp about a month, I guess, when we had mail call one day," Bryan recalled. "I got a letter and saw from the return address that it was from a high school buddy of mine named Leo Fenili. I was happy to be getting mail from him. It was nice to know that I wasn't being completely forgotten out here, you know. I opened the letter and it was in the first line. Something about how he couldn't believe that Tim had been killed, and wondering how I was handling it. I couldn't believe what I was reading. He obviously just assumed that I had already known. I freaked out! I remember that there was this special procedure that you had to perform before a recruit was allowed to enter the drill instructor's quarters if you needed to speak to him. I was in no mood, or state of mind, to go through all these motions, but I also knew that I'd never get it to talk to him if I didn't follow the rules. Three hard bangs on the outside of the entryway and then formally announcing myself to the DI -- identifying who I was and the reason for my desire to enter his office. After doing this whole routine, I was finally allowed permission to call home and get the news from my dad. The nonstop intensity and strain of the boot camp training never allowed me any time to feel sorry for myself, or really do any mourning for Tim. What did weigh on me very heavily was that when my training was over that I, too, was going to have to go to Vietnam."

CHAPTER NINE
CONCESSION

"One of the hardest things I ever had to do was to go over to that house." Bob Dillon said. "We sat in the kitchen with Lubitza drinking coffee. She was more worried about what might happen to Bryan, rather than talking about Tim. I knew I had to go into the living room to talk to Michael, but for a long while I just couldn't bring myself to do it."

"Our friends and neighbors really came together to support us in those first few days and weeks," Ellen Fitzmaurice Shea said. "The front door was always opening with someone coming by to drop off food, expressing their sorrow, and offering to help with whatever we needed. Mrs. Dillon, Bryan's mother, was especially supportive, bringing over food and talking with my Mom. Mrs. Dillon had so many of her own children at home to care for, and yet she still took the time to come over and try to bring some kind of comfort to our family."

One of the most trying aspects of the Fitzmaurice family's ordeal was the fact that even after the death announcement it was still another week before Tim's body could return home for burial. There were, of course, funeral plans to be made, and that work kept Lubitza somewhat occupied. But in between making the funeral arrangements and greeting the guests who came to the house, the pain surrounding Lubitza was obvious. "My Mom was thoroughly devastated," daughter Maureen recalled. "Even at my very young age, that was easily apparent to me. I found out later from Jack that my Dad took some consolation in the fact that Tim died alongside his brothers as he called them, his fellow Marines. Dad knew that Tim wasn't alone when he died. That had to be something that only someone who had known the worst of war could take comfort in."

Lance Corporal Timothy Fitzmaurice's body eventually made it home on Thursday, May 23, 1968. The flag-draped casket was met at the airport by Marine Corps Sergeant Donald Conner. Sergeant Conner was a wounded Vietnam veteran whose job as casualty escort was to stay with the body of Tim Fitzmaurice at all times, and to attend to any needs of the family until the burial was completed. Tim's older sister, Ellen, looked back, "I think the Marines chose Sergeant Conner because he was Irish. They probably had an idea that my Dad might be more comfortable around a fellow Irishman during those days." Tim's body was brought from the airport to Tohle Funeral Home on Lawrence Avenue, just around the corner from the Fitzmaurice house. Michael wanted a three-night wake for his son. The funeral home advised him that it was not usually done for there to be a wake of that length, and convinced Michael to scale back his desire to the more customary two-night service. "I remember how heartbroken I was to hear that Lubitza had wanted to go up to that funeral home to see Tim's body one last time. She didn't know that it had to be a closed casket, and that she would not be allowed to view Tim's remains," Bob Dillon recalled.

Father Gerald F. Mulcahy from Saint Edward Parish would preside over the funeral service. Father Mulcahy and Tim had been friends since Tim's high school years, and the two had

CONCESSION

exchanged letters during Tim's time in the Marine Corps. Father Mulcahy brought great comfort to the Fitzmaurice family by being at Chicago's O'Hare Airport to meet the airplane that had brought Tim's body back home. Father Mulcahy asked for Michael and Lubitza's permission to use Tim's service as a time to try out something different for the Mass of Remembrance. The priest explained to the family that instead of wearing the traditional colors of mourning, black and purple, he wanted all the colors to be white -- the priests' vestments, the casket draping, and the church memorial bunting. This funeral mass was not to be a mourning of death, instead it would an inspirational celebration of life. The Fitzmaurice family quickly embraced the idea.

Chicago newspapers were calling the Fitzmaurice house constantly. They wanted the thoughts from yet another Chicago family whose son hadn't come home alive from Vietnam. There were a lot of those stories to write in May of 1968. It would end up being the deadliest month in the entire war for American military personnel. Timothy Fitzmaurice was one of 2,415 soldiers, sailors, airmen, and Marines who made the ultimate sacrifice in Vietnam during May, 1968. Chicago newspapers were particularly busy with tales of death and tragedy, as 56 Chicago boys perished during that deadly month. The story of Tim Fitzmaurice's life and death would go untold at that time, however, as Michael and Lubitza refused to talk to the media about the loss of their beloved son. This grief they would keep to themselves.

Six Marines served as the pall bearers who carried Lance Corporal Timothy Fitzmaurice up the steps of Saint Edward Church. These same steps had seen Tim's baptism, first holy communion, confirmation, and eighth grade graduation. Previously, the steps had seen the caskets of other Saint Edward Parish servicemen killed in Vietnam -- Michael Badsing, Donald Sansone, John Cronin, and one month after Tim's funeral, another dead Marine would cross the threshold of Saint Edward Church. Corporal Richard Ray Machut, Delta Company, First Battalion, Fifth Marine Regiment was killed on June 17, 1968, in Thua Thien Province. Corporal Machut's brother, Lieutenant Colonel Roger Machut, United States Marine Corps, remembered Richard. "He was my idol, a Marine, 14 years older than me," Colonel Machut said. "He was on patrol, and they were ambushed. He took a grenade round to the mid-portion of his body. It blew his legs off, basically from the waist down. We were told that he didn't suffer long. He lived about a half-hour after that. I remember it all -- being informed, seeing my parents suffering, waiting for two weeks for Richard to come home and the wake. I remember those days distinctly. I've lived with his memory and wanted to be like him."

The Vietnam War would cause two more servicemen to be brought to Saint Edward Church for funeral services before the conflict's end. Corporal Patrick Edward Poppenga, Alpha Company, First Battalion, Fifth Infantry Regiment of the 25th Infantry Division, was killed on June 5, 1969, in Binh Duong, South Vietnam. Mary Hansen, a high school classmate of Patrick's from Schurz High School in Chicago, remembered him, "We graduated together in 1967. The years have escaped all of us, especially all of those on The Wall who left us so very early at much too young an age. It was a time of much turmoil when Patrick left for Vietnam. Thank God our servicemen and women now get more recognition than the Vietnam veterans ever received. It's never too late to thank them for their service and giving their lives for us. I hope he has been resting in peace. God bless him." And finally there would be Warrant Officer Ralph Dulane Tadevic of Charlie Company, 227th Assault Helicopter Battalion, Eleventh Aviation Group of the First Cavalry Division. Warrant Officer Tadevic was shot down and killed in Vietnam on October 28, 1969, in Phuoc Long Province. A flight school classmate, Richard Muirhead, remembered Ralph, "After we got our orders we shipped out to Vietnam on April 6, 1969. I sat next to him on the flight to 'Nam. I was assigned to the First Aviation Brigade and he was assigned to the First Cav. The next time I saw his name in print was in the Stars and Stripes newspaper, on that list that no one wanted to make. I want to thank him for being my friend and for making the ultimate sacrifice for our country. I will never forget him."

When the time came for Father Gerald Mulcahy to give the eulogy at the funeral mass of Tim Fitzmaurice, the priest spoke eloquently of service and sacrifice, of courage and commitment, of selflessness and dedication, but mostly he talked of love -- Tim's love for his parents and grandparents, his brother and sisters, and all his friends. He also had a great love of country and his brother Marines. His deep love for his fellow Marines was what led to this day. Timothy Fitzmaurice volunteered for Vietnam so another Marine wouldn't have to go in his place. He said as much in his letter to his girlfriend, Cindy, when he told her of his decision to go to Vietnam. Tim would not allow his dreams to be assured, while others put their own futures at risk.

Tim's devastated family sat in the front pews enveloped in inconsolable sadness. Grandpa Soraich was quietly sobbing. Grandma Soraich was not permitted to attend the funeral mass. She was suffering from very high blood pressure -- the stress brought to her by the week's events required that she remain home on bed rest. Michael Fitzmaurice, although weak and frail from his own ailments, tried valiantly to be strong for his despairing wife, Lubitza. Ellen and Jack were sitting stunned and heartbroken. Young Maureen was confused and scared, not knowing what to think -- was Timmy really inside that casket? When the funeral mass had ended, the mourners lined up for the procession to Queen of Heaven Cemetery. There, the final words were said over Tim's body in a chapel ceremony. On a beautiful May morning a 21-gun salute was fired. Before the flag was removed from the casket, a lone bugler player Taps as the assembled family and friends bowed their heads in an agonizing final prayer. The flag was then folded into the traditional triangle formation before being presented into the trembling hands of a tearful Lubitza, with these words spoken by the flag bearer: "On behalf of the President of the United States, the Commandant of the Marine Corps, and a grateful nation, please accept this flag as a symbol of your son's service to country and Corps". While the gathering solemnly and slowly began returning to their cars, a bagpiper was heard wailing in the distance. The Fitzmaurice family were left to stare silently at the casket before saying their final goodbyes. Timothy Fitzmaurice's final resting place was to the right of where his parents, Michael and Lubitza, would eventually be buried. Tim shouldn't have been there before they were. This wasn't how it was supposed to be.

The day continued with a luncheon back at the Fitzmaurice home on Kewanee Avenue. Close friends and family gathered to tell stories and remember. They tried to recall a time before the war, when young men were allowed to grow up and grow old with their dreams. They told funny stories of Boy Scouts and ball games, of playing in the yard and Sunday drives, of work and church and family and love. But while the enduring memories were being beautifully retold, there were also feelings of anger and remorse and disbelief and resentment.

"It was the first time that I was exposed to commentary that changed the way I dealt with my memories of Tim and the grief I carried." Ellen said. "Even on the day of Tim's funeral, there were some who could not refrain from letting myself and my brother, Jack, know their feelings about the war, and the worthiness of Tim's service and death. Jack and I were suffering under the weight of all this sadness, and in Jack's case, tremendous guilt as well, but there were some people who wanted to use that particular time to tell us that Timmy never belonged in Vietnam, and that his death was a waste. The insensitivity really shocked us. I realized that it was a byproduct of the times in which we were living. It was May of '68. There was no end in sight to the war and I remember a friend of mine saying that all she recalls about

Vietnam were the never-ending stories of young men dying."

Jack Fitzmaurice in his junior year photo from the DePaul Academy yearbook of 1966.

Eventually, the friends and relations began to head home. They were heading back to their lives and leaving the Fitzmaurice family alone with their new reality. They paid their respects to each

Fitzmaurice family member before they left. They embraced Michael and Lubitza with sincere offers of assistance should anything be needed. Last to leave was Sergeant Donald Conner, Tim's Marine Corps casualty escort. The Marine had done his duty. He had seen to it that the body of one of his fallen brothers had been honorably and respectfully laid to rest. Before leaving the Fitzmaurice home, Sergeant Conner looked back to see what remained of the family that he had helped through a tragedy -- Grandma and Grandpa in a tearful embrace, Ellen, Jack, and Maureen retreating to the silence of their rooms to deal with their confusion and heartbreak. Michael was sitting in his chair, putting on his oxygen mask and turning on the evening news. The strength that he had mustered through the preceding days was all gone. He stared blankly at the television -- there was more news from Vietnam. Lubitza was busying herself cleaning up the last of the coffee cups and the desert plates. The day couldn't have been real -- did she really just bury her son? Her home would never again be filled with the sound of Tim's voice, his songs, his jokes, his stories, or his laughter. She loved him so much and now he was gone, and with him went the life she had once known. The calamity of Vietnam had come home to Kewanee Avenue, and when Sergeant Conner finally turned to leave the Fitzmaurice family, he left behind so many more casualties than just the Marine he had helped lay to rest.

CHAPTER TEN
ISOLATION

"When my Mom said goodbye to me, she didn't think that she would ever see me again." Tim Fitzmaurice's high school friend, Len Swiatly, left for Vietnam in October of 1968. He was a United States Navy Seaman Recruit stationed on the *U.S.S. Jennings County*, a support ship for river gunboats patrolling the backwaters of South Vietnam. "I had attended Tim's funeral and, for me, it was the first time that I had lost anyone I was close to. It was a shock. It wasn't too long in the past when all we were concerned about were girls and beer. Now guys were coming home dead and wounded and really messed up. And for those of us who were heading to Vietnam, well, I can't speak for everyone, but Vietnam scared the hell out of me."

The Fitzmaurice family had to deal with two heartbreaking deliveries to their door in the days following the funeral and burial --Tim's personal effects arrived at the house on Kewanee Avenue. The first delivery came direct from the field of battle in Vietnam. The Rosary and Miraculous Medal that Lubitza Fitzmaurice had lovingly, and hopefully, placed into her son's hand before he left for the war, had now been returned to her. Battle dress fatigues, and boots caked with the mud of Hill 1192, were pulled from a duffel bag, as well as Tim's utility knife. That weapon was first purchased for Tim by Michael Fitzmaurice, with specific guidelines from his son. The knife had to be a

Ka-Bar, which was the popular name for the combat knife first adopted by the United States Marine Corps in 1942. Michael would later present the knife to Dennis Shea for use during Dennis' own tour of duty in Vietnam. The second package to arrive at the Fitzmaurice home was from Okinawa. Inside was Tim's green, Class "A" Marine Corps dress uniform. The family's last vision of Tim was when he was wearing that uniform on the day he left for Vietnam. Mom and Dad, Ellen, Jack, and Maureen had all posed for pictures with Tim in his "greens" before he proudly left home to serve his country. He had only said goodbye to his family a few months earlier, but with his uniform returned to them, Tim was now gone forever.

The turmoil surrounding the war and its effects only heightened in the weeks and months after Tim Fitzmaurice's death. Only two weeks after Tim's funeral, Senator Robert F. Kennedy was assassinated in Los Angeles, California. After having won the California Democratic presidential primary, Senator Kennedy was giving his victory speech in the ballroom at the Ambassador Hotel. Shortly after midnight on June 5, 1968, Kennedy was shot as he walked through the kitchen of the hotel, and died in Good Samaritan Hospital some twenty-six hours later. Kennedy had mentioned in his victory address in Los Angeles how excited he was to be heading to Chicago to campaign for the upcoming Illinois primary to be held on June 11. The assassination and its aftermath once again thrust Chicago into the eye of the storm of the burgeoning anti-war movement -- not only because of the importance of the Illinois primary in the wake of Kennedy's death, but more pointedly, the Democratic National Convention was going to be held in Chicago in August. The whole world would be watching as the streets of Chicago became the scene of riotous behavior. Anti-war demonstrators faced off against members of the Chicago Police Department. Thrown into the volatile mix was the

ISOLATION

presence of Illinois National Guardsmen, utilized by Chicago Mayor Richard J. Daley to maintain law and order during the convention. The streets of Chicago exploded under the pressure, when the demonstrators and the police clashed with each other under the watchful eye of a national television audience. The war that had torn at the heart of the Fitzmaurice family was now tearing at the heart of a city and a nation. The flag of the National Liberation Front, more commonly known as the Viet Cong, was being flown by young protestors in Chicago's own Grant Park. Some of the agitators were even burning the American flag. For families who had already lost loved ones in Vietnam, the scenes were hard to endure. Michael Fitzmaurice watched the chaos from his living room on Kewanee Avenue. Why were these college kids acting in this way? Didn't they appreciate Tim's sacrifice? How could they so cruelly trample on the memories of those who had given their lives in Vietnam?

SMILE ON YOUR BROTHER

Another Chicago Marine's family felt that exact same pain and torment. Lance Corporal Michael Derrig, Echo Company, Second Battalion, Ninth Marine Regiment, was killed in Quang Tri Province on August 27, 1968. It happened to be the second day of the Democratic convention back home in Chicago, and Michael's father, Police Sergeant Philip J. Derrig, was manning the barricades in Grant Park during the anti-war protests. Sergeant Derrig was summoned to his West Side home to hear the news of his son's death, yet the next day he put on his Chicago Police uniform and returned to work at the barricades. Sergeant Derrig's son, Philip, Jr., recalled: "When Dad was told of Mike's death, he got tears in his eyes and put his arm around my mother and said: 'It'll be all right.' But there was always something missing after that. We were blue-collar kids from blue-collar families, and all of us knew we were facing the draft. Our parents were children of the Depression. They didn't figure that the world owed them a living. Dad said the first couple of days in Grant Park that he couldn't understand why the college kids did what they did. But he didn't hate the protesters. He did his job. He was a professional. I just wish that we had been able to separate the warrior from the war, and taken better care of our soldiers when they came home from Vietnam."

Young people were rising up in protest against the war in general, and the draft in particular. College campuses were a hotbed of anti-war rebellion and dissent against those who served in the military. Tim's sister, Ellen, recalled: "After Tim's death the protesters made me angry. Jack and I were in school at DePaul University and it was easy to spot the military kids on campus. The way they dressed, the length of their hair -- in many ways they stood out. There were a lot of times that I heard other students talk about how military kids were stupid. It was so hard to have to listen to that. The sacrifices that these guys had made wasn't being respected at all. In fact it was just the opposite. They were ridiculed for being in the military and for having served in Vietnam. That type of thinking permanently altered my attitude about dealing with memories of Tim. I wouldn't speak of his death until I had known someone for a long time, and only then if I trusted that they would respect what my whole family was dealing with. There were so many ignorant comments about 'baby killers' and other vile criticisms about the guys who were coming back from Vietnam. I just couldn't deal with a lot of that, so I kept my brother's death to myself and I grieved in silence."

Experiences were very similar for Tim's brother, Jack. Jack Fitzmaurice was a freshman at DePaul University when Tim was killed. On campus, Jack was battling with some of the same torments that were plaguing Ellen. Inability to deal with these emotions would be one of the primary reasons that prompted Jack's final decision to leave college.

There were other issues at work, but they were all derived from the fact that Jack had lost his brother in Vietnam. Jack's wife, Maureen Dillon, said that Jack rarely spoke of his deceased brother, but one description of the pain that Jack admitted to had always stayed with her: "When Timmy died, my life ended too." College and all it had to offer was no longer Jack's life path. Whether it was his disgust for the tone and tenor of collegiate life that was prevalent at the time, or that Jack's father's health was in continual decline, and that Jack could better serve the family by working full time and bringing home the money, Jack left school, never to return.

What was commonly felt when it came to opinions about Jack Fitzmaurice's life, was that he carried around a heavy burden of guilt. The origin of the guilt was not that easy to pin down, however. After Tim was killed, Michael and Lubitza wanted Jack to apply for "sole surviving son" status -- it was a military policy set forth to protect members of a family from the draft, or from combat duty, if they had already lost family members in military service. Jack very reluctantly acquiesced to his parents' wishes, because, despite what his family had already been through, Jack still saw military service in his future, and would have gone to Vietnam if called upon. The fact that so many of those he knew and grown up with had served in Vietnam, made the self-imposed guilt of not having served that much harder on him. In many ways, Jack's guilt could be termed "survivor's guilt." He was spared the test of serving his country by a brother who had made the ultimate sacrifice. Tim's girlfriend, Cindy Koenig Moderi, saw some of the same things from her perspective. "I think Jack did have guilt from the 'sole surviving son' status, and it stemmed from the fact that he thought he had something to prove to people. I never got that about Jack. There was nothing to prove to anyone. But I don't think that he saw it that way." Jack's brother-in-law, Dennis Shea, recalled one of the discussions that the two of them had about Tim. "Jack had seen a television program about some of the difficulties that Vietnam veterans were experiencing as they were re-acclimating themselves to civilian life after their wartime service. Flashbacks, Agent Orange exposure, Post-Traumatic Stress Disorder, and other issues were just starting to surface at the time. Jack said a very interesting comment to me after having seen that program. 'Tim would have been all messed up if he'd made it home.' I asked him what he meant by that. Jack knew that Tim had been in some horrifying combat situations during the war. He knew his brother better than anyone, and was sure that even had Tim made it home that he would have carried the trauma of Vietnam with him always."

For Michael Fitzmaurice and his wife, Lubitza, the loss of their son was borne silently. "We wouldn't talk to them about Timmy. There were no conversations. I never heard them talking to each other about him either," Ellen said of her parents. "My mother was very religious, and it was her faith that she leaned on to try to get her through those first few weeks and months after Tim's death. The outpouring of love and support that was shown to our family was truly overwhelming. People were so generous to my Mom and Dad, and it meant so much to us. But it's natural that people have to go back to their own lives. You quickly come to the realization that you are on your own in dealing with grief. The weight on my mother's shoulders had to have been incredible. My Dad was 62 years old when Timmy died, and his health was declining rapidly. Jack and I were very busy with our own lives. My mother had my Grandma and Grandpa downstairs, and my ten-year-old sister to care for, but she had to have felt very alone in her pain." Lubitza was only 48 years old at the time of her son's death. All the qualities and attributes that had made her such a joyous person before Tim was killed, were overshadowed now by an aura of sadness and hurt. As her daughter, Maureen, recalled, "The pain and grief in the house was consuming. I would spend the weeks following Timmy's death just trying to stay out of everyone's way. But it was obvious to all of us that a piece of my Mom died too, that day in May."

Sadly for the Fitzmaurice clan, the reality remained that the Vietnam War would still be a traumatic family presence in the years to come. Ellen had met and fallen in love with a fellow DePaul University student named Dennis Shea. Dennis, who was born and raised on the northside of Chicago, was the son of Irish-immigrant parents. He was a 1964 graduate of DePaul Academy High School, and then entered DePaul University to begin his collegiate studies. During his junior year in college, he met Ellen Fitzmaurice and it was love at first sight. Dennis saw Ellen at the university's nearby train station and struck up a conversation with her. He boarded the train that was taking Ellen home, even though it was going in the opposite direction of where he needed to go. He didn't stop there either. Ellen connected to the rest of her trip home via bus, so Dennis boarded the bus as well, further distancing himself from his own trip home. It just took him that long to finally get Ellen to agree to go out with him for their first date. It wasn't long before they were seeing each other seriously. Of course, everything was serious about those days in 1967 and 1968. The futures of many young people seemed so precarious. Dennis was enrolled in the Reserve Officer Training Corps (ROTC) program at DePaul University. Ellen was very familiar at that time with military commitments. Her brother, Tim, had already been in the Marine Corps for a year when she started seeing Dennis, so beginning to care deeply for someone whom she knew would eventually have to leave for a long period of time in order to satisfy his military obligations, was something that Ellen was willing to accept. The realities of service in Vietnam were still a long way off for both her brother, Tim, and for her new found love, Dennis. There would be plenty of time and opportunity to worry about Vietnam later.

Dennis Shea only had a few encounters with Tim Fitzmaurice before Tim left for Vietnam. "I have a couple of memories that stick out in my mind. I phoned the Fitzmaurice home one time early on in our courtship, and I asked to speak with Ellen. On leave for a week or so from the Marine Corps, Private Tim Fitzmaurice answers the phone. Never having met each other, we go through a two-second drill of 'hi, how are 'ya' and so on. Tim then puts the phone down, and ever so clearly announces -- not so softly, but loud and clear -- 'Ellen, your fool's on the phone!' That's how I first met Tim. Now two nights later, Ellen and I are sitting near the top of the front steps at 4740 Kewanee Avenue, and a car pulls up. Out he comes. But I can't see him because it's dark, about 11:00 PM or so, and he's moving in a blur. He's coming up the wooden porch steps two at a time. I expect him to stop, and he does, for only about two seconds. Here it comes -- the greeting. I'm about 20 years-old and Tim was 19. I didn't really expect any sincere greeting. All I'm really expecting is a quick 'hi', but I also thought that he might hit me with the same treatment that I got on the phone a couple of nights earlier. Something like, 'Hi, I'm Tim, you must be the fool.' So he slows for a moment and utters an indiscernible word or two, and moves into the house. I'm thinking 'whew,' but I'm also thinking, 'who does he think he is? He doesn't have time to talk with me and his sister?' It was only much later, in a chat with Jack, that I put it all together. Dad Fitzmaurice had imprinted the wrath of the curfew law on his two sons -- even at home on leave, Tim had better be in the house by 11:00 PM or he would hear about it from his father. Tim was serving in the Corps, keeping peace abroad, but he also knew what he had to do to keep peace at home."

In August of 1968, three months after Tim's death, and right in the middle of the anti-war upheaval that was gripping the streets of Chicago, Dennis Shea left for Officer Basic School with the United States Army. Before he left, Ellen gave him a sapphire ring as a sign that they were committed to one another. Not an engagement ring, but more a symbol of hope. Hope that as Dennis began the journey that would eventually lead him to Vietnam that, unlike Tim, Dennis would somehow find his way back to Ellen. It was unthinkable that this war would take two people whom she loved so dearly. Vietnam couldn't do that to her again, Ellen reasoned. So she gave Dennis a ring, a sign, to come back home, and to have a life with her. The ring symbolized that Dennis was not alone on this journey. They would make this trip together -- if he could just survive.

"I remember thinking to myself at the time that Ellen was trying to force my hand, to move me toward engagement faster than I had planned. But I had to put myself in her shoes. She and her family had suffered an indescribable loss only three months earlier. She was under no illusions about the dangers that were ahead of me. I was young and gung-ho, and although I had been there for Ellen during the time of Tim's death, I still carried that air of invincibility that only youth brings. Ellen was well past that point in her life now -- she knew better. Vietnam robbed her of her youthful innocence when it took her brother."

Dennis Shea graduated from DePaul University in May, 1968. Having spent his college years in the ROTC program, he was commissioned a second lieutenant in the United States Army on June

12, 1968. Just five weeks after Tim's death, Ellen, along with Dennis' mother, Bridget, was there to pin the second lieutenant rank on to Dennis' uniform. In August of 1968, Dennis left for Armor School at Fort Knox, Kentucky. He graduated from the armor course in November, with Ellen in attendance. His first duty assignment was at Fort Bliss, Texas, as a Training Officer. In June of 1969, Dennis left for Camp Davis in the Panama Canal Zone for ten days of jungle training. Then, in mid-June, he shipped out to the Republic of South Vietnam to begin his year of duty. Lieutenant Dennis Shea was assigned to the 199th Light Infantry Brigade, initially as a platoon leader with D Troop of the 17th Cavalry. Later he would serve as the brigade's assistant intelligence officer. Dennis recalled, "My impending service in Vietnam just added to the overwhelming burden that Tim's death had brought to the family. I only realized that after the fact, because during those terrible days of mourning, I still didn't get it. The fact was that I, myself, would cause a great deal of worry to this family, including Grandma and Grandpa Soraich. I was heading to Vietnam just a year after Tim's death, and so were some of my, and Ellen's, college friends. Those were difficult days."

The seriousness of the times required that important decisions not be put off until tomorrow. Ellen and Dennis were in love, but the specter of Vietnam hung over their love, and made their future together uncertain. Dennis wanted to propose marriage before his deployment to Vietnam. Tradition and decorum dictated that he would have to go to Ellen's father, Michael, for permission to ask for his daughter's hand in marriage. Michael would have to bless the engagement of his daughter to a man who would shortly be leaving for a combat assignment in Vietnam. The situation was stark. Vietnam had taken Michael's son, and now Dennis was about to head into harm's way. There was also a reality that Michael knew all too well from his World War II service. No one comes back from war the same person as before. War changes you, one way or the other. Frail and weak, Michael Fitzmaurice struggled to rise from his chair to shake hands with Dennis and give his blessing. After the engagement, Ellen went around to meet Dennis' relatives. The meetings were tempered by the fact that Dennis was also using this occasion to say goodbye to his family before leaving for Vietnam. The engagement served as a safe topic to focus on, as everyone tried not to think about the war. The wedding itself would take place after Dennis' tour was over. "He'll be back in a year and we'll get married then," Ellen hoped. One piece of wedding business had to be decided upon before Dennis left. The wedding reception hall had to be booked many months in advance. Ellen and Dennis made it a priority to find a nice place, but with one overriding provision -- it had to be a reception hall that would return any monetary deposit should Dennis not make it home from Vietnam. That particular caveat turned out to be more of a challenge than expected. What is the policy on returning deposits to the fiancées of dead soldiers? Only one place, called the Fontana D'Or, agreed to a full refund of any deposit. The wedding reception would be held there. With a dream, and a plan to begin a life together when he made it back, Dennis said goodbye to Ellen. Their farewell was two days before Dennis' departure. He spent his last days at home with his family. Ellen and her parents encouraged the decision for Dennis to spend his final days home surrounded by his mother, Bridget, his father, Dennis, and his sister, Mary Catherine. Dennis and Ellen talked frequently on the phone those last couple of days. They talked of love, and war, and Tim, and their future. Then Dennis left for Vietnam.

For Ellen and the rest of the Fitzmaurice family, the cycle of despair and fear would begin again. There were letters back and forth, followed by

ISOLATION

intense worry should one of Dennis' letters home arrive late. Ellen wrote almost every day, talking a lot about family and her continued teaching work. Dennis wrote back, speaking in general terms of day-to-day life in Vietnam. He was very careful not to get too specific about the dangers that being in a combat zone brought to an Army infantry platoon leader. Dennis was very sensitive to the feelings of his fiancée and her family who had recently lost someone so dear to them. Dennis kept much of his war and the perils that it held to himself. He loved Ellen too much to make her have to re-live Vietnam through his experiences there. The year passed slowly.

Vietnam came calling for Tim Fitzmaurice's friends as well. Len Swiatly was Tim's high school classmate from DePaul Academy. Len got a spot in the United States Navy Reserves right after graduation. However, through a series of unforeseen events, and some paperwork mishaps, Len eventually found himself in the active duty Navy. His tour in Vietnam began in October of 1968. "When I left for Vietnam, I remember my mother thought, mainly because of Tim's death, that she would never see me again. She was thoroughly convinced that I wasn't coming home, and believe me, she had me pretty well convinced also. Going to Vietnam scared the shit out of me." Len was stationed on the *USS Jennings County,* a tank landing ship used to conduct and support river patrol operations. These operations were an attempt to deny the Viet Cong access to the resources in the Mekong River Delta area of South Vietnam. "Between Tim's death and my own introduction to Vietnam, I grew up fast. It was quite an awakening. When I got home from the war, there was a small group of family and friends who truly appreciated my service, but I also had to deal with some unfortunate incidents. I did get spit on, wearing my whites, walking through the airport in Los Angeles. There are so many who have no concept of what service to this country means, and

ISOLATION

what it takes to preserve our freedoms and way of life. I'm 62 years-old now, and I would do it all again in a heartbeat."

Len Swiatly pictured with captured Vietcong flag, aboard his ship the USS Jennings County.

One month after Len Swiatly left for Vietnam, Bryan Dillon's orders came through. By November of 1968, the war had been going on for three and a half years. A new president, Richard M. Nixon, had been elected with a platform that promised a "secret plan" to end the war in Vietnam. The antiwar movement was at its zenith, with college campuses and city streets swarming with protesters calling for an end to our country's involvement in Vietnam. American dead were coming home from Indochina in staggering numbers. In May 1968, the month Tim Fitzmaurice died, there were 2,415 G.I.'s killed in action, 1,310 dead in June, 1,009 were killed in July, 1,214 dead in August, 1,230 dead in September, and 805 more U.S. servicemen were killed in action in October of 1968. This was the reality of the times, this was the devastation that the war had brought home in the six months since Tim Fitzmaurice's life had been taken. This was the war that Bryan Dillon was heading to in November of 1968, and as Bryan's mother, Pat, took her first born child into her arms in the moments before he would leave her, she, too, didn't know if she would ever see him again. When the car taking Bryan Dillon to his airport departure slowly drove away from the Dillon family home, he was leaving the safety and protection of his mother's love. Pat Dillon was standing on the sidewalk with her heart breaking. She turned to go back into the house, and saw the faces of her nine other children staring at her. It was a defining moment. She realized that there were too many who counted on her strength to let them down now. Her worry and suffering over Bryan and the war would have to be kept inside, hidden from view.

In the car ride to the airport, Bryan and his father, Bob, passed the time with nervous chatter about the weather and who was going to take care of Bryan's car while he was gone, and how the house wouldn't be so crowded for awhile until he got back. The focus was always on things that would happen when Bryan got home. Vietnam was just going to be something that they had to get past before things would get back to normal. Bob Dillon shook his son's hand and watched him board the plane on the first leg of a long journey, taking Bryan to the war that had already killed his best friend.

Bryan Dillon carried with him a gift from Tim Fitzmaurice's mother, Lubitza. The gift was the medal that Tim had worn during his time in Vietnam. It was the very same "Miraculous Medal" that Lubitza had given her son on the day Tim left for the war. Death was a possibility for Bryan, and no one knew that quite so clearly as Lubitza. She wanted for Bryan the same protection that she had hoped the medal would have brought to her own son. In the Roman Catholic tradition, special graces were to be granted to the medal wearer at the hour of his death, through the intercession of the Blessed Virgin Mary. Lubitza's son was gone, and now she was trying to shield Bryan from the dangers that she knew awaited him. So she gave him Tim's medal with a note that partially read, "This medal may not have helped Tim, but may you be blessed by wearing it."

ISOLATION

Bryan Dillon pictured in Vietnam wearing the same Miraculous Medal worn by Timothy Fitzmaurice. The Medal was given to Bryan by Lubitza Fitzmaurice.

The initial stop from Chicago on Bryan Dillon's transport was Hawaii. From there a plane took him to the island of Okinawa, and the home base of the Third Marine Division. Bryan was stationed on Okinawa for a week before boarding the plane for his final destination -- Danang Air Base, Republic of South Vietnam. "The flight over from Okinawa to Danang was pretty upbeat, guys talking and laughing," Bryan recalled. "But when we landed, and the doors on that plane opened up, the talking and the jokes stopped."

First stop in Danang was the receiving tent where the newly arriving Marines received their duty assignments. Bryan was headed for a unit in Quang Tri Province, six miles south of the Demilitarized Zone that separated North and South Vietnam. His outfit was the Headquarters and Service Company (H&S), Third Medical Battalion, of the Third Marine Division. The Headquarters of the Third Marine Division operated in Vietnam beginning in May of 1965, with elements participating in operations from Danang to Phu Bai and up to the Quang Tri / Dong Ha Combat Base. Over their four years of continuous combat operations, the Third Marine Division lost more than 3,000 Marines killed in action.

Dr. Albert Naar was a surgeon in the United States Navy Medical Corps, and was stationed at the Third Medical Battalion during Bryan Dillon's time there. "The Medical Battalion was logistically located in a bad place because most of the fighting had moved up north to our area during that time. Wounded would be flown to the base by helicopter. The doctors treated many different kinds of wounds, such as shrapnel wounds, bullet wounds, and head wounds, and performed amputations. When the choppers landed, the most seriously hurt patients were taken off first. The patients would then go to triage which was organized chaos."

Bryan Dillon and his fellow Marines stationed at the Third Medical Battalion would meet the incoming helicopters on the tarmac, off load the wounded personnel, and get them into triage as fast as possible. When the choppers weren't coming, time was spent filling sandbags, or riding shotgun on re-supply convoys bound for remote Marine outposts and firebases.

"We'd take shifts of eight-hour watches, but the job was round-the-clock," Bryan remembered. "It was all hands on deck when the wounded arrived. The call often went out for blood donations from base personnel. Unfortunately, there never seemed to be enough blood for all that was needed." The battalion suffered through its share of mortar and rocket attacks. Bryan's duty also included manning posts for perimeter security, protecting the base from North Vietnamese or Vietcong sapper attacks. Enemy activity around the base was frequently encountered, and air strikes and artillery were brought in to clear out the NVA and VC positions. A particularly effective use of American air power against Communist forces advancing against the base perimeter was provided by "Puff the Magic Dragon," an AC-47 gunship. Cruising in an overhead orbit at an altitude of 3,000 feet, the gunship could put a bullet into every square yard of a football field-sized target in less than ten seconds. As long as the plane's load of ammunition held out, it could bring this devastation on to the enemy while loitering over the area for hours.

"I started out strong sending letters home, letting everyone know that I was OK and that things were going fine," Bryan Dillon recalled. "But as the weeks turned into months, I didn't write as often. I regret not writing more. I'm sure that not hearing from me for weeks at a time had to be hard on everyone."

One particular incident brought that reality home in a serious way. Bryan was sent to Saigon, the capital of South Vietnam, for additional training relative to his military occupational specialty. While in Saigon, his appendix ruptured and he had to be rushed into emergency surgery. After surgery in Saigon, Bryan was sent to the United States Military Hospital at Cam Ranh Bay, South Vietnam. While recovering there, an infection set in that was serious enough to put Bryan's life in jeopardy. Because of this dire situation, Bryan had to be evacuated to the United States Naval Hospital in Yokosuka, Japan. After almost three weeks in the Naval Hospital, much of that time spent in the intensive care unit, the infection was finally brought under control. Bryan, however, had been out of communication with his family for over a month. Bryan's parents were overcome with worry, and his mother, Pat, decided to get in touch with the American Red Cross to see if she could find out any information about her son. She was finally able to connect with Bryan while he was in his last days of recovery in Japan. The relief at hearing the sound of her son's voice was indescribable for a mother who had feared the worst. Pat Dillon was calmed to hear that her son was okay after the weeks-long appendix ordeal. But after Bryan's full recovery in Japan it was back to Okinawa to wait for his ride back to Danang, and then on to resume his duties with the Third Medical Battalion.

The reality of his friend Tim's death could have given Bryan's own tour of duty in Vietnam an ominous feel. "There's something about being young. I didn't think that could ever happen to me. I was bulletproof. I talked about Tim with some of the other guys I served with. I told them everything that happened. But we couldn't, or wouldn't, focus on that kind of thing. We all just wanted to do what we had to do and then get home. You know, I hated the thought of having to go to war. I lost my best friend and I experienced some terrible things.

But it was the defining time in my life, and I was immensely proud to have served. I knew when I got home from Vietnam, though, that things would never be the same."

CHAPTER ELEVEN
CONTINUATION

The mourners had stopped coming by the house on Kewanee Avenue. The flowers, the condolence cards, and the meals weren't showing up at the front door anymore. Everyone had to return to their old lives. But for Grandma and Grandpa Soraich, for Michael and Lubitza, for Ellen, Jack, and Maureen, there was no longer an old life to return to. Their lives moved forward, but now there was a emptiness to it all. The sadness and heartache brought on by Tim's death, and the continuous decline in Michael's physical condition, made life at the Fitzmaurice house very somber. There were, however, some moments of joy that came to the family. By June of 1970, Dennis Shea had made it home safely from Vietnam. Meeting him at the airport for his welcome home were his mother, Bridget, his sister, Mary Catherine, and, of course, his fiancee, Ellen. Ellen remembered the phone call she received from Dennis telling of his imminent arrival home from Vietnam. "He gave his flight details, and let me know that his mother and sister would be there as well to greet him. I remember that I told him that he should go straight to his mother first. He didn't need that reminder, but I wanted him to feel comfortable as this was a very emotional time for all of us. The plan was that he would return to his own home to be with his family after the airport. His father was waiting for him there, and they all spent the day together. Dennis then came over to our house that night. My grandparents and Jack and

Maureen were very happy to see him. My parents were happy as well, and both of them were very relieved to see that Dennis was home safe and healthy. They never said anything to me, but I wonder if that day also brought painful memories to them that they never had a chance to welcome Timmy home."

Bryan Dillon also made it home safely from Vietnam. His 13-month tour ended in December of 1969. He made his way to the San Francisco airport after stops in Danang, Okinawa, and Hawaii. The final leg of Bryan's trip home would be an eventful one, however. A little more than one hour into his flight from San Francisco to Chicago, it was reported that there was a fire in one of the plane's engines, and that there would have to be an emergency landing in Tulsa, Oklahoma.

The plane landed without further incident in Tulsa, but the situation brought nervous laughter to some of the other returning servicemen on board. The irony of surviving Vietnam, only to fall victim to a malfunctioning commercial airliner somewhere over Oklahoma, had many of the military men heading into the airport bar in Tulsa to await their next flight. Bryan caught his follow-up plane to Midway Airport in Chicago, where he and a few other veterans decided to ride home in style from the airport by hiring a limousine. When the limo pulled up to Bryan's house he exited the car and then paused for a moment. He turned to look at the front door of the home that he had left over a year earlier. So much had changed inside him, but as he looked at his house, and then up and down the street, so much had stayed the same around him. It was a challenge faced by many of our nation's warriors returning home from the battlefields of Southeast Asia. They would have to reconcile their searing experiences in Vietnam, with a civilian world that was more interested in putting Vietnam aside. Bryan entered his home to an emotional reunion with his parents, and his brothers and sisters. It was a low-key homecoming, with feelings of immense relief overshadowing any sense of celebration. Bob Dillon recalled: "We had never discussed the possibility of something happening to Bryan. We just put our faith in God and prayed. I guess we had a feeling between us that it wouldn't have done any good to worry each other over it. We lived through watching what had happened with the Fitzmaurice family. We didn't need any other reminders."

The plight of the Vietnam veteran was unique among the experiences of those we, as a nation, sent to war. The country was in turmoil about the conflict itself, and about those whom we sent to fight it. For many veterans who had served in Vietnam, the stories were tragically similar. In all but a small group of family and friends, their service was, at best, ignored and, at worst, openly denigrated as disgraceful and, possibly, criminal. Most disheartening for a lot of the returning veterans was the treatment received from the veterans of our nation's other conflicts of World War II and Korea. Incredibly, some Vietnam vets were told upon returning home that they had not fought in a "real war." A deeper wound was when those of a previous generation of veterans believed that some of the well-publicized atrocities from Vietnam were indicative of the entire wartime effort of the Vietnam veteran. It was the ultimate betrayal to have other veterans believing that Vietnam-era servicemen had somehow disgraced the uniform. This feeling ran so deep that the organization called the *Vietnam Veterans of America*, chartered in 1978, had as its founding principle, "Never again will one generation of veterans abandon another."

This was the America that Dennis Shea, Bryan Dillon, Len Swiatly, and 2.5 million other returning Vietnam veterans, came home to. Len Swiatly reflected on the disrespectful treatment he was shown upon his return, "When I think about getting spit on at Los Angeles Airport, it was such a shock that it rendered you immobile and disbelieving. It was only after I had some time to think about what happened that the anger really set in. My friend, Tim, was killed before I even left for Vietnam, and I went over there thinking the same thing might happen to me. But I went anyway, and came back incredibly proud of my service there. And then that thing happens at L.A. Airport and I just couldn't comprehend being treated that way." The message was received loud and clear by the returning vets: keep your service and your stories to yourself. After having returned from Vietnam, Bryan Dillon recalled that there wasn't a lot of interest from extended family on where he had been, and the things he had seen. "That's just not the way it was back then." The Vietnam War had begun to tear away at the fabric of our society. The country was showing indifference to service, and duty, and honor, and in the process, disrespecting the memories of those who had made the ultimate sacrifice.

It was the essence of those times that added to the heartbreak that the Fitzmaurice family was struggling with. How did a family lose a loved one in Vietnam and not be able to speak freely of the pain being endured? How did a family mourn in a time when not everyone shared in respecting the magnitude of their loss? Tim's younger sister, Maureen, tried to make some sense out of the conditions that existed in the country at that time. "Being so young, I was not aware of the climate that existed, and the nasty, rotten things that people had said to Ellen and Jack after Tim died. They lived the Vietnam era in a completely different way than I did. The war was on television every evening, but if it weren't for Timmy, and the following year Dennis, it would only have been a news story to me. Ellen and Jack knew a lot of people who were affected by the war. I didn't. To my friends, as I got older, Timmy was a hero and someone to look up to. I often wonder how different our lives would have been if Timmy came home to us after his tour of duty was over. I know that Jack would have had a happier life and made different life choices. I know that Mom would have been different and Dad's health would not have deteriorated so quickly. While Ellen would have still worried and prayed for Dennis to come home safely, she wouldn't have had the added pain of knowing just how bad it was over there. Maybe she would have had an easier time when letters were delayed? As for me, I'd like to think that my childhood would have gone on a little longer. I would have lived in that blissful space where bad things don't happen for just a while more. But that didn't happen, and Timmy was taken from us too soon. He became our Guardian Angel, and I believe that he still looks over all of us."

The difference between generational attitudes toward the service of the Vietnam veteran could not have been more defined. Why did Jack and Ellen Fitzmaurice have to endure so much insensitivity and disaffection when attempting to come to grips with the tragic loss of their brother? What changed in the subsequent generation whereby Maureen could rightly and openly perceive her brother, Tim, as a hero, and someone to be unreservedly admired? Of course the war in Vietnam was detested by huge segments of the American populace, but so were the wars in Iraq and Afghanistan. Why was so much of the hatred for the war in Vietnam directed at those who were sent to fight? Vietnam veterans were not asked if they wanted to go to war, they didn't have a vote. They were directed to go to war and they went. These were people, many of whom who thought that they would not make it home, who willingly went to Vietnam to serve their country. There was a compounding effect to the grief that the Fitzmaurice family was dealing with after the loss of Tim. To lose a loved one in war is tragic enough, but when many refuse to value or respect the service that precipitated the loss, then the wounds of grief can never fully heal.

In October of 1970, there was a respite from the anguish that had dogged the Fitzmaurice's since Tim's death. Ellen Fitzmaurice married Dennis Shea in a ceremony at Saint Edward Church. Their first date had taken place on April 15, 1967, and the road to their wedding day had not been a normal courtship. There was tragedy and sorrow, fear and worry, loneliness and grief. But what always triumphed over those difficult days was their courage and love, which could never be defeated. They relied on each other, and they counted on each other to make it through the agonies of war and loss. It was truly a love strengthened through adversity. When they stood at the same altar that had seen Tim's casket only two years earlier, they were already intimately familiar with the marital vow of sticking together through the good times and the bad times. More than forty years later, they remain true to that promise.

Standing on the altar with them that day were Ellen's bridesmaids. One of the women was Ellen's good friend, and her brother, Tim's, girlfriend, Cindy Koenig. Cindy had stayed close with the Fitzmaurice family even after Tim's death. She attended DePaul University with Ellen and Jack. "Ellen and I were sorority sisters at DePaul, but I also considered her a big sister in life. We had become very close, and I think that the fact that we were both feeling this tremendous loss brought us even closer." Ellen and Cindy remained in close contact for many, many years after Tim's death, with Cindy having Ellen stand up in her eventual wedding as well. Over the years, the demands and obligations of work and family would gradually lessen their contact with each other, but they would always carry a special bond in their love for Tim. Cindy also kept in touch with Jack Fitzmaurice, even after Jack had left DePaul University. There were mutual friends and social connections that frequently brought them together. Cindy saw the changes that Tim's death had brought to Jack. "Jack was devastated after losing Tim. He just wasn't the same person after that. He seemed to be weighed down by this tremendous guilt that he was carrying. Tim and Jack had very different personalities, but I liked Jack. We both had a lot in common -- we both loved Tim and missed him very much." Cindy recalled an incident that happened between her and Jack which brought the mutual pain that they were dealing with to the forefront. "I can't remember how long Tim had been gone when I saw Jack at a DePaul party one evening. He walked in wearing an Irish sweater that I had made and given to Tim as a Christmas present the year before he left for Vietnam. I can still remember just how mad I was to see Jack in Tim's sweater. I went right up to him and in a very emotional voice told him that it was Tim's sweater, and it was a special Christmas gift that I had made for him, and that Jack had no right to be wearing it. I insisted that he take the sweater off right then and there. I could tell how embarrassed he was. He left the party. Looking back I could see that we were both just missing Tim and dealing with our sadness the best we could. Jack just wanted to be wearing something that reminded him of his brother, and I wanted Tim's memory to be honored so much that Jack wouldn't think of wearing a gift that had so much emotion attached to it. Yes, the sweater belonged to Tim, but it was also *mine and Tim's*. It was a memory that we had shared, and Jack wasn't respecting that. It was a small example of how difficult those early months and years of loss were on everyone who loved and missed Tim."

Michael Fitzmaurice died on September 3rd, 1971. He was only 66 years of age, but the ravages of emphysema, and the remnants of his World War II injuries, had combined to take their toll on the proud Irish patriarch. He had once struggled to comfort his own family with the thought that his son, Timothy, had fought and died alongside his military family, his brothers-in-arms, and that notion was to somehow bring peace to a devastated household. Michael, more than anyone, knew the realities of war and the horrors that emanated from it, but that knowledge was no protection against the heartbreak of losing his son in Vietnam. With his spirit broken, his physical deterioration accelerated quickly after Tim's death. In a way, death may have been a release for Michael from the chains of disease and despondency. Life had never been easy for Michael, starting with his hardscrabble childhood on the streets of Chicago's westside. This proud son of Irish immigrants knew the darker side of life. He went to war as a man in his late thirties and was badly wounded. His daughters remember a father who was often sick and in pain. The pain, as it turned out, would be as much emotional as it was physical. Whether it was the lingering effects of the shrapnel that he carried around in his body, or the onset of emphysema that would slowly rob him of his ability to function, life for Michael Fitzmaurice was a long travail. But it was the death of his son, Timothy, in Vietnam that made it all so unfair. Michael had already been through too much to deserve to have his son taken from him. Near the end of his days, as he tried in vain to sleep sitting upright in his chair, he had to wonder why so much hardship had befallen him. It would have been a logical thought, even for the most devoutly religious among us. The funeral procession for Michael Fitzmaurice led from the steps of Saint Edward Church to Queen of Heaven cemetery. The mourners watched as Michael was laid in his final resting place next to Tim's grave. He was reunited now with the son he had loved so dearly.

"Dad died on my first day of high school," Maureen recalled. "He had been sick for a very long time, but that didn't make it any easier. Thirteen years of age is not a good time to lose a father, especially after losing Timmy when I was just ten years old. I don't know how my Mom handled it. I'm a mother and the thought of losing one of my children, well, I just couldn't even imagine it. On top of that, to have to work all day and then come home to a very sick husband -- the strain must have been intolerable. She was an incredibly strong and supportive mom. We never talked about the emotional weight she was carrying. Those were subjects that were left alone. Each day was a struggle. I miss her terribly."

Losing a brother and father before starting high school can't help but harden a person to the cruelty of life's realities. Severe illness, war, and death are big issues for a young girl to grapple with. "My childhood was definitely a short one," Maureen recalled. "If Timmy had made it home, I would have had another big brother to help me get through life. Timmy could have been there to help us all."

But it was the life plan of Jack Fitzmaurice that saw the biggest alteration when is brother, Tim, didn't return from Vietnam. In the fall of 1967, while Tim was standing a post in Guantanamo Bay, Cuba, Jack began his undergraduate work at DePaul University. It was a pivotal time for each brother. Jack was forging ahead with his college coursework, which he hoped would shape his future, and his brother was about to make his decision to volunteer for duty in Vietnam. Two teenage brothers who had different visions of what the immediate future had in store for them. Jack was an English literature major during his time at DePaul University. He had once given the name of *Ethan Frome* to a Fitzmaurice family cat. He also had a keen interest in mathematics and business. Those particular courses were offered at a different DePaul University school location, in downtown Chicago, several miles south of the school's main campus. Ellen remembered that the two school locations had other differences as well, besides geography. "The DePaul uptown and downtown locations were very different, both in what classes were taught and the general tone and environment. For whatever reasons, Jack witnessed much more hostility directed at the students who were returning veterans when he was attending classes downtown. I remember Jack befriending a vet and bringing him home to visit with the family. The student told us that he felt very isolated at DePaul. He was very comfortable with Jack. He gave my mom some ideas on what to send to Timmy, and he was kind enough to come to the wake. I believe that Jack eventually left DePaul for several reasons. He only had a year and a half more to complete his degree, but the emotional stress that he was dealing with made it impossible for him to continue his studies. He was intensely uncomfortable with the campus attitudes towards veterans. He was already dealing with the trauma of losing Tim, but he just couldn't handle seeing the disrespect being shown to others who came back from serving in Vietnam."

For Jack, the time had come to put the two and a half years he had invested in higher education behind him. There once may have been a thought of following his sister, Ellen, into the teaching profession, but those dreams were put away now.

There was a new reality of life without Tim and the immediate ramifications that that fact now had on the Fitzmaurice family. A job working construction became available to Jack. His parents needed financial help at home. Steady work and ready money were right at hand. No more uncertainties about a future career path. No more everyday reminders at DePaul of the ingratitude for his brother's sacrifice. Jack took the construction position and left school and all of its possibilities behind.

Michael Fitzmaurice's death had concluded four years of emotional trauma and personal tragedy for his wife Lubitza. Her only sister, Militza, had died in September of 1967. Lubitza had lost one of her true confidantes when her sister passed away. Eight months after Militza's untimely passing came her son, Tim's, death. It was a heavy burden to bear -- working full-time to support her family, caring for an infirmed husband, and raising a ten-year-old daughter. After her husband

Michael's death loneliness and sadness began to take hold of Lubitza. She was only 51 years-old when she lost her husband, but the cumulative effects of the personal tragedies that she had endured in the preceding years had taken a severe mental and physical toll on her. Lubitza was always being counted on to be strong. When she lost her son, Tim, she still had to be there for her husband and children in their suffering. When her husband, Michael, passed away, she had a young daughter and elderly parents who needed her strength. "My mother was the most amazing woman," Maureen lovingly recalled. "She was so strong and caring and forgiving and supportive. I still feel her presence in my life every day." In time, Lubitza Fitzmaurice tried to resume some activities and interests that freed her from some of the responsibilities of home life. She became more social, going to dinner with friends and involving herself even more deeply in parish activities at Saint Edward Church. But it was the artistic side of Lubitza that was able to show its expression in the years following her husband's death. She began to paint. She painted in oils, acrylics, and water colors. She was quite an accomplished artist, and many of her paintings would become gifts for special family occasions. Ellen and Maureen still have some of their mother's artwork hanging in their homes. Lubitza had always been a multi-talented, multi-faceted person, and painting provided her with comfort.

In 1973, Ellen Fitzmaurice Shea gave birth to her first child, Timothy. Ellen and Dennis named their son after a brother whose life had been taken in Vietnam five years earlier. The birth was a breath of fresh air for the family. The arrival of the new baby brought happiness and laughter back into the lives of the extended Fitzmaurice family. It was a renewal. Life wasn't always about sickness and death -- there could be joy. The birth of her first grandchild had shown that to Lubitza. After losing her sister, her son, and her husband in the previous six years, the birth of Timmy Shea confirmed in Lubitza the faith that she had held so dear -- the miracle of life and the possibility that it holds. Tragically, those positive feelings would be short-lived for Lubitza. Her beloved mother, Anna Soraich, passed away after a short illness in 1975. It was just another devastating blow to Lubitza and the rest of the family. Throughout all of the hard times and tragedy that had taken place with her family on Kewanee Avenue, Lubitza always knew that she had a loving mother who resided right downstairs to comfort and support her. Now Anna was gone, and Lubitza once again felt the ache that comes with loss and grief. She lost her mother, the one person whom she didn't always have to be strong for; the person whom she could be herself with and, if only for a few moments each day, let down her guard enough to say that life was hard and it was not always easy to keep going. It has been said that no one is truly the same after losing one's mother. The one person you knew who loved you unconditionally is gone from your life, and nothing can ever fill the void that is left behind. Lubitza Fitzmaurice had known intense emotional pain, but losing her mother joined that pain now with abiding loneliness. At the same time, however, she knew she had to put her own feelings of grief away for the sake of her father. Her father needed her now more than ever. Ilija Soraich was still a vibrant man - the force of his personality naturally drew people to him. He thrived on the nightly conversations that he would have with his daughter. He looked forward to those evening chats with Lubitza to stem the feelings of despair that the loss of his wife had caused. Also, Grandpa Soraich was increasingly tormented by the fact that he had now buried his daughter, Militza, his wife, Anna, and his grandson, Tim. Lubitza would sit with him every night for a couple of hours just to talk with him and reassure him. Thankfully, there was a new addition to the extended family as Ellen and Dennis welcomed the birth of their second son, Michael, in 1976. It was always a much needed break from the everyday routine when Ellen dropped by Kewanee Avenue to bring the two babies to see Grandma Lubitza and Great Grandpa Ilija.

Maureen Fitzmaurice married David Schiesser on May 20, 1978. They married at Saint Edward Church. Maureen's wedding day filled a church that had seen so much Fitzmaurice family sorrow, with elation. "Leaving Kewanee Avenue was bittersweet for me," Maureen remembered. "Grandpa still lived on the first floor and Mom and Jack still lived upstairs. It was the only home that I had ever known, and at the ripe old age of twenty I was pretty young to be married and out of the house. I visited often and it was always home. I had my first kiss on that front porch. I laughed with friends, cried with girlfriends over boys, fought with boyfriends, sat out on the steps on warm summer evenings, and dug out cars on snowy winter days.

Dave asked my Mom for my hand in marriage in that living room. I got ready for my wedding in that house. I brought my first born child home to Kewanee Avenue when she was released from the hospital. Sure, we had hardships and terrible grief while I lived there, but we also had love. My mother loved us all totally and completely, and did everything she could to make sure we were happy and felt her love."

Lubitza Fitzmaurice's enormous capacity for love had sustained her and, combined with her faith in God, carried her through some of the most difficult days imaginable. But in the summer of 1980, it was her physical strength which had started to fail her. Lubitza had been feeling unusually run down and fatigued. She knew something was not right with her health. She had always been so vital and active, and the loss of her physical stamina became very disconcerting to her. Without informing the rest of the family, Lubitza went to see her physician for a full battery of tests, and when she received the results her world was once again shaken to the core. Lubitza was diagnosed with colon cancer and her doctor informed her that the cancer was in an advanced state. A woman, who had lost her only sister, her first born son, her husband, and her mother in a hideous eight-year span, had now received her own crippling diagnosis. Yet, remarkably, Lubitza's Catholic faith held strong in the midst of these never-ceasing tragedies. Ellen Fitzmaurice Shea recalled those days: "It was a philosophy that our whole family came to embrace to try to get through the hard times, and it came directly from Grandma and Grandpa -- there's a plan and we are not in charge. Grandpa called it "God power." You have to remember, Grandma and Grandpa were farmers before they immigrated to this country. So many factors were out of their control when it came to their success at farming. They had known severe hardship and they were tough and resilient people, and I believe that they did their utmost to try to pass that toughness on to all of us."

Lubitza would, once again, be a shining example to her family as she battled cancer in the year following her diagnosis. The cancer determination was such a cruel blow to Lubitza, coming at a time when some joy was returning to her life. Two more grandchildren came into the family. Maureen's first child, Laurel, arrived in September of 1978, and Ellen's third child, Dennis, was born in early summer of 1980. With four grandchildren and her many parish activities to attend to, Lubitza had some happy moments to take her away from the waves of sadness that would sometimes wash over her. She was only 60 years old when given the news of her cancer. She was still working full time and was socially engaged. She was a doting grandmother and spoiled her grandchildren shamelessly. She had been through so much, but there was more that she wanted to accomplish with her life. It would have been a natural reaction to wonder how her cancer diagnosis could be part of any plan. Yet Lubitza refused to let bitterness or self-pity consume her. She waged her cancer battle with the most powerful weapon that she had at her disposal, her faith.

For Lubitza's daughter, Maureen, it was the cumulative effect of all of life tragedies that may have been contributing factors to her mother's illness. "I believe that severe stress can trigger all types of biological issues in our bodies. And my mother's life was stressful. An ailing husband unable to work, worries about money, losing her son to a horrible war -- these were just a few of the reasons that stress became a constant presence for her." Lubitza's first born child, Ellen, also witnessed her mother's struggles. "I realize that many of us get a turn at tragedy in our lives, but my mother's life was so hard. And, without a doubt, losing Timmy in Vietnam was the hardest thing of all for her."

Lubitza Fitzmaurice places a memorial bouquet into the waters of Lake Michigan at the conclusion of a ceremony honoring Chicago servicemen killed in Vietnam.

Medical science seems to corroborate the feelings of Ellen and Maureen. The detrimental effects of stress on our overall health cannot be understated. "A causal link between stress levels and various cancers is constantly being researched, and while the studies are new, inflammatory pathways activated by stress have been implicated in the development of tumors, metastasis of tumors, and resistance of chemotherapy," said Dr. Charles Raison, Professor of Psychiatry and Behavioral Sciences, and Director of the Behavioral Immunology Clinic at Emory University in Atlanta, Georgia.

Lubitza Fitzmaurice died on July 21, 1981, at the age of 61. It can surely be said that one of the contributing factors to her death at such a young age was the Vietnam War. Since that tragic day in May of 1968, Lubitza carried the anguish of losing her son, Timmy, with her for the remaining days of her life. The pain consumed her from the inside out until she had nothing left to fight against it. Her immune system was overwhelmed by her level of sorrow. With her defenses worn away she became susceptible to disease. Grief and torment take their toll just as surely as physical afflictions do. Just because the marks of emotional trauma are not visually evident doesn't mean that they aren't the ultimate contributors to one's decline. The Vietnam War was continuing to claim victims. Lubitza's story is one of a life given to courage and sacrifice. As a younger woman, she watched as the man she loved went to do his duty for his country. Michael Fitzmaurice came back to Lubitza a different man, permanently changed by the physical and psychological wounds that he bore. Because of that, Lubitza's life was changed as well. She gave her first born son to her country in another war, and when he didn't return to her, the life she had, and the life she hoped for, was gone.

Lubitza Fitzmaurice's funeral brought her to her beloved Saint Edward Church for the last time. The church that had become such an integral part of her life would be the place of her final goodbye. Considering that Lubitza was a convert to the Roman Catholic faith, it was clear that Saint Edward Parish had lost one of its most ardent disciples. The priest's sermon tried to bring comfort to her family. Lubitza was now in the hands of God, with whom she had bravely faced life's pain. For Lubitza's children it was difficult to understand why a woman of tremendous faith could be burdened by such crippling heartache. It is a common refrain on why good people must sometimes see so much suffering. The answers are never clear. But as they buried Lubitza next to her husband, Michael, and her son, Timothy, her suffering had ended. It would now be left to her surviving children to make their way in the world without their cherished mother. What she left to them was an inspiring example of a faithful perseverance lived with grace and courage even when life had turned its darkest.

CHAPTER TWELVE
CONNECTION

The Fitzmaurice children were settling back into their lives, and working at healing. Ellen and Maureen were busy with their growing families, but Jack Fitzmaurice was by himself now. He was the last of the family to be living in the upstairs home on Kewanee Avenue. Grandpa Soraich was still downstairs, and Jack became an extremely attentive caretaker for his grandfather. Jack had begun seeing a woman by the name of Maureen Dillon who worked in the office of Jack's construction firm. Maureen was born in Brooklyn, New York, and raised in neighboring New Jersey. She had come out to Chicago to work on her undergraduate studies, and stayed on after graduation. In 1982, Maureen and Jack married. The wedding ceremony took place in Maureen Dillon's home town back in New Jersey. The newlyweds came back to Chicago and found an apartment. Before leaving the home on Kewanee Avenue, however, Jack had to make considerations for Grandpa. Ilija Soraich was not getting any younger and he had come to rely on Jack for so much. The family was very fortunate to find a friend of a neighbor who was happy to rent the upstairs apartment after Jack's departure. The new renter grew to become a great companion to Grandpa Soraich, dining with him at least once a week and checking in on him daily. Knowing that Grandpa was being well cared for was a great source of comfort for Jack.

In August of 1985, Maureen gave birth to their son, Liam. It was the most joyous time in Jack's life. As young Liam grew, Jack was there by his side as soccer coach, softball coach, and Scoutmaster. Jack loved being involved in his son Liam's activities, and was always there for every event in which Liam participated. Yet, as pleased and contented as Jack appeared to be to others, there was always something just beneath the surface that would not allow for his total happiness. "He was a very guarded person," his wife, Maureen, recalled. "And I remember kind of a tell tale sign of where he allowed his mind to go when he told me that, 'Tim had missed out on having a family life. He was never able to have any of this.' That was the guilt Jack carried with him." Jack couldn't really embrace all that he had because his brother, Tim, was not there to have the same experiences.

The Fitzmaurice family absorbed another blow in September of 1987 when Ilija Soraich,

Grandpa, passed away. It had not been a surprise; in declining health for years, Ilija was 96 years old at the time of his death. Grandpa Soraich was the family's last link to their past. Ilija had come to America, like so many immigrants before and since, with a dream to pursue happiness through freedom. What he painfully learned over his long lifetime was that attaining his dream would not come without cost. A price had to be paid, and sadly, Ilija and his family rendered a heavy toll. Ilija's son-in-law, Michael Fitzmaurice, had been badly wounded in North Africa during World War II. Those wounds, both mental and physical, led to a lifetime of repercussions for Ilija's daughter, Lubitza, and her family. Ilija then had to watch his grandson, Tim, go off to war and never return. The impact from that tragedy stayed with Grandpa Soraich until his final breath. He had lived to see the deaths of his wife, his two daughters, and his grandson, and the pain of losing those he had loved so dearly had disheartened him. But Ilija took comfort in the same axiom that he had tried to impart to others to get through the bad times -- it is all part of a plan that God has for us. After 96 years, Ilija had, indeed, followed God's plan. When Grandpa's time of departure had come, he and his family knew that he had lived the tenets of one of his favorite bible verses -- Ilija had "fought the good fight, finished the race, and kept the faith."

It was a severe bout of rheumatoid arthritis that forced Jack Fitzmaurice to take an early retirement from his construction firm. He simply became unable to perform the work required of a very physically demanding job. The additional free time that the retirement allowed did not turn out to be a healthy inclusion to Jack's life. Occasionally prone to immoderate alcohol consumption during his working life, Jack's drinking began to worsen. As his moods darkened, he became much more emotional. "He was always very guarded with his emotions, but as he got older he began to let his guard down more and more," his wife Maureen recalled. "It always came back to his feelings on losing his brother. It was heartbreaking to see how the guilt that Jack carried around just tore him up inside."

Jack Fitzmaurice

Jack Fitzmaurice died on July 7, 2007, at a hospital near his suburban Chicago home. After suffering through a series of medical issues that had severely weakened him, he succumbed to organ failure at the age of 58. He left behind his wife, Maureen, and his 22 year-old son, Liam.

It is an interesting thing -- war and its aftermath. The Vietnam War may have ended many years ago, but its effects have spanned generations. Each name etched on the Vietnam Veterans Memorial Wall represents family members who had to come to grips with lives diminished. How those family members dealt with death is the ripple effect that continues to make the Vietnam War such a huge part of the American landscape. Drugs, alcohol, depression, severe stress, divorce, suicide -- these were not issues relegated only to returning servicemen. They are everyday realities for those who are still bravely trying to absorb the losses of loved ones, long after the war has ended. Death may have been an end to the suffering for those heroes whose names grace the Vietnam Wall, but it was only the beginning of the suffering for the heroic families who had to cope with those losses. There is no national memorial for those casualties of Vietnam. Lubitza Fitzmaurice was only 61 years old when she died, and her son Jack passed away at age 58. Can it not be said that they died, in part, because of complications from the emotional wounds that they both received that horrible day in May, 1968?

For Tim's sisters, Ellen and Maureen, their brother Jack's death was just another in a series of devastating emotional blows. Once again, these incredibly strong women had no choice but to go on, but they could not help but feel that they were losing parts of themselves as their beloved family members kept disappearing from their lives. They chose to forego self-pity and instead put their focus on the raising and nurturing of their own families.

Ellen Shea gave birth to another child one year after her mother's death. Son, Bryan, rounded out a family of four boys for Dennis and Ellen. She quickly went back to working full time as a teacher in the Chicago Public School system. It was good to be busy and focused on her husband, her work, and her growing family. The preceding years had been so stressful and emotionally difficult for Ellen. It was time to try to put those sad memories to the back of her mind, and devote her energies to work and family. Ellen had been raised well by her own parents. Michael and Lubitza had taught her to handle the hardships that life dealt out by leaning on faith in God, and love, for the help needed to get through the difficult times. She raised her sons as her brother, Tim, had been raised: Catholic school, altar boys, athletic events, and Boy Scouts. But, thankfully, times were different now. The military draft had long since been abolished. Ellen did not have the same worries as her mother had grappled with, of young sons going off to war leaving behind terrified and distressed parents. Military service was still a huge part of family life for Ellen and Dennis. Dennis remained an Army Reservist after his service in Vietnam had finished, eventually rising to the rank of Colonel. But the military was not something that was going to be forced on to their sons. "They were free to make up their own minds about serving," Ellen said. "But, being honest, military service for any one of them would have been terrible. Having my own children gave me a perspective on what my mother must have been feeling. I simply could not imagine sending one of my sons off to war."

Ellen's sister, Maureen, expressed some of the exact same sentiments. After her first daughter, Laurel, was born, there came two more daughters, Kristin and Kathleen, followed by son, Michael. "I remember after Michael had graduated high school he was contacted by a Marine Corps recruiter to obtain information on a possible enlistment." The Marine recruiter followed up with a visit to Maureen's home to provide the requested information. Unfortunately for the young Marine, his home visit was met with the impassioned response of a mother who had lost her brother in Vietnam, and was not about to let her only son take his turn in the Corps. "I was pretty vocal with this guy. I wanted him to get the idea that there was no way that my son was going to go into the Marines. I told the recruiter all about the impact that Timmy's death had had on our family, and that there was no chance in hell that I'd allow that happen to my family. After he left the house, I kind of felt sorry for the guy, but my emotions had pretty much taken over, and I felt that I had to let that man know what I had been through."

So Ellen and Maureen live their lives and, together with their devoted husbands, have raised their families. Their children know that there is a place in their mothers' hearts where sadness and hurt survive, and a place where lives that could have been, reside. Together, as family, they work to remember. Every year on May 9, the anniversary of Tim's death, they visit the gravesite where Tim lies alongside his parents. Always when they arrive at the grave, Ellen and Maureen see that someone has been there before them. They know this because of the presence of fresh flowers atop Tim's gravestone. Though the flowers had been left without a card or name attached, the Fitzmaurice family have always known in their hearts that they were put there by Cindy Koenig Moderi. It gave the sisters comfort to know that someone who had known and loved Tim was still thinking of him and remembering him in this way.

Cindy and Tim were just kids back then, before Vietnam. They had their hopes and their dreams, and the gravesite flowers were Cindy's way to remember that those hopes had meaning, but the dreams weren't allowed to come true. The flowers were also a symbol that, although she had made a happy and purposeful life for herself, with a loving husband and children, Cindy never would forget the plans of two young people with faith in each other; ready to take on the world together, before Vietnam changed everything.

CHAPTER THIRTEEN
COMMEMORATION

On Saturday, March 10, 2012, a funeral was held for a Marine from Chicago who was killed in action in Afghanistan. Lance Corporal Connor Thomas Lowry, born and raised in the southside parish of Saint John Fisher, gave his life for his country on March 1, 2012. He was a proud young Irishman loved by family and friends. He had a personal motto that guided him through his many life experiences, "Live Life Large." Connor did just that for all of his twenty-four years. The funeral mass celebrant, Reverend Quinn Conners, spoke of Connor's dedication to family and his desire to serve others. "He stepped up with pride and loyalty. He was part of that Marine Corps family that we have seen in evidence so many times. He took a vow of generosity to defend freedom and liberty for us, and for people thousands of miles away. He also vowed to care for his family, and particularly his mother. They were not only mother and son, but were best friends." Others who knew and loved Connor Lowry were also allowed to say a few words. They talked of a man with a great sense of humor, which drew others to him by the force of his personality. They let you inside on the agonies of a family who had a loved one in harm's way. The family had tried to remain positive during Connor's deployment, but fear and apprehension were always there. Before he left for Afghanistan, Connor told his sister Grace, 'I love you', with the most meaning I had ever heard," she recalled. "I didn't think he would die."

At the wake, mourners wound their way through the packed church before viewing Connor Lowry's body. There was an inspiring Marine Corps presence at the service. Marines were everywhere, standing guard, consoling attendees, and showing support for one of their fallen brothers. As those who came to honor Connor got closer to the end of the line to view his body, the raw emotion of the situation began to grip them. Ahead of them were the stunned faces of Connor's brothers and sisters, and the crushing tears of his grieving mother. The mourners could not help but be overcome by the sheer display of the family's courage. As with the Fitzmaurice family so many years before, the memorial was only the beginning of a family's battle with pain and loss. For Connor Lowry's family, the war in Afghanistan will never have an end. It will always be there, every day that they live without Connor.

Those who came to pay their respects shook Connor's mother's trembling hand, and mouthed the words that Lubitza Fitzmaurice had no doubt heard countless times during those trying days around her son Tim's funeral, "We're sorry for your loss." Many said those words while feeling the intense emotion of the moment, but without any true idea of the meaning of the word "loss." There is simply no way to quantify what is lost when a young person is taken. Lost is the promise that Connor's life could have offered to those who loved him. He could have been an inspirational husband and father; he could have been the brother who was leaned on when life got rough; he could have been the friend who was there to help make it through the hard times. You take notice throughout your life of every moment, good or bad, when you wish he were there, and as the years go on without him you begin to gain the full measure of the meaning of the word "loss."

By attending the memorial services of heroes such as Lance Corporal Connor Lowry, there is an attempt to gain a greater understanding into the personal struggles that overwhelm all military families who suffer through their ultimate sacrifice. It is impossible, however, to know the depth of their pain without having walked in their shoes. Hats are removed and hands placed over hearts at ballgames when the National Anthem is played, and emotions are stirred at hearing Taps played at Memorial Day ceremonies, but so many know nothing of the words "ultimate sacrifice." When that sacrifice is personified in the courageous family members of the fallen, it is genuinely humbling. Because their sacrifice isn't just the loss suffered by a loved one on the field of battle, but it is the lifetime of sacrifices shared by the family members who grieve forever.

It has been forty five years since Timothy Fitzmaurice was killed in Vietnam. Those who knew and loved him have lived their lives without him. They have married, raised their families, and grown older, while trying to come to terms with what was lost all those years ago. It is a fact of the human condition that loved ones are sometimes tragically taken, forcing those who loved them to go on much differently than before. But when someone so young, with so much promise, is lost all that remains from the loss are the possibilities of what life could have offered if only that person could have stayed for just a while longer. 58,267 Americans never made it home from Vietnam. As devastating as that death toll truly is, that number is just the beginning of the story. When you take into account that the fallen had mothers and fathers, sisters and brothers, wives and children, friends and girlfriends, and so many others who loved them, it is evident how the ripple effect of grief leftover from Vietnam still envelops our nation. The despondency being felt by the Fitzmaurice family has revealed itself all across this country and shaped an entire generation.

There was a television news program in August of 2009, celebrating the 40th anniversary of the Woodstock Music and Art Fair. On the program panel members were each trying to gauge the broader significance of the iconic festival to see if the values and ideals of the festival attendees still had relevance today. One of the commentators went on to say that "an entire generation had come of age in the mud of Woodstock." There were varying degrees of acquiescence exhibited by some of the other panelists, but one pundit's remark remained long after the show had ended. "Some of them may have come of age in the mud of Woodstock, but I venture to say that many more of them would tell you that their generation truly came of age in the mud of Vietnam." Vietnam took a generation's childhood, its innocence, and, for many, it took their optimism as well. Death has a calamitous way of destroying those ideals. The future challenge, however, lies in not unfairly placing this despair on the shoulders of the following generation. Tim Fitzmaurice's sisters, Ellen Shea and Maureen Schiesser, have been about the business of raising the next generation of children following Vietnam. What is the legacy that they have tried to impart to their children? What can those who lived the horrors of Vietnam teach to subsequent generations?

Ellen's husband, Dennis Shea, commented on the coincidental timing of the various aspects of Tim Fitzmaurice's story coming to light now. So much new information was surfacing aided by the Internet and the research being done by Dennis and Ellen's own children that it now felt like the right time. "History has a way of revealing itself many years after the fact," Dennis opined. The essence of Dennis' observation weaved its way through all of the stories of the people who lived through those turbulent times. Family, friends, and war veterans have needed to put time and space in between the events of those tragic days, and their ability to try to put it all into perspective for a more thorough understanding of what they had lived through. Our country itself was also going through a more detailed self-examination. Vietnam veterans, and their sacrifices, were getting a second look. The children of these veterans were growing up and telling the real stories of the men and women that they knew. Their parents were loyal, dedicated, hard-working, and fiercely patriotic. The veterans, incredibly, spoke of their willingness to do it all again, despite all that they had seen and been through, despite the treatment that they had received upon their return home from war, despite the mischaracterization and criticism of their Vietnam service. Despite all of that, if given the same choice again, they would serve proudly and without hesitation. It is that special quality that makes the Vietnam generation of warrior truly unique. In many ways their country turned its back on them, but they never turned their backs on their country. In an interesting turn of events, there have been several recent attempts by political candidates to go so far as to fabricate their military service records so that they could claim to have served in Vietnam. Where once Vietnam veterans had to hide their service records in order to increase their chances at being accepted, it has now become a resume highlight to have served in Vietnam.

Another fascinating aspect of America's newfound admiration for the Vietnam veteran was relayed by Arthur Bresnahan, a Fitzmaurice family friend, and a Marine Corps helicopter pilot veteran of Vietnam. Art confessed to encountering a surprising number of men of his age group who, for whatever circumstances, did not have to serve in Vietnam, and now regret not having done so. Art Bresnahan stressed that many of the men he had spoken with told him of their moral and political opposition to the war; how they felt the war to be a waste of young lives and a grave mistake for our country. Yet, there was something deep down inside of these men that gnawed at them about Vietnam. Their brains told them that serving in Vietnam would have been insanity, and to be avoided at all costs. But somehow now, even knowing the outcomes and the tragedies, their hearts still can't completely let go of Vietnam. Many of these men are angry with themselves for holding on to their feelings of guilt for not having served. Why does Vietnam follow them still? Might their feelings emanate from the same place as the sincere words written by a 19-year-old Tim Fitzmaurice to his girlfriend, Cindy? "There are many things in this world that I want -- a good education, a good job, a family, and you. But not if other people have to die for it to be that way."

Maybe those men remember all of those who took their turns in Vietnam and never made it home -- the ones who never knew the love of a wife and children. There are over 58,000 ghosts who haunt us all even today. They come in and out of our lives at different times to remind us that there is a price to pay for all that we hold dear. That is why Tim Fitzmaurice's family and friends remember him, and they tell his story, and they make sure that those who will follow them remember as well. A brother, a friend, a love, is gone from their lives far too soon, but he is carried in their hearts to call on whenever they need him. The legacy remains as it has always been -- never forget.

AFTERWORD

I received a call from Bryan Dillon on Saturday, November 7, 2010. The Fitzmaurice family's old Chicago neighborhood, Mayfair, was having a "Salute to American Heroes Day," and one of the day's honorees was going to be Tim. Bryan asked me if I'd like to join him for the memorial ceremony. The event was sponsored by the local Lions Club. According to their organization, "The Mayfair Lions Club was chartered in 1947 when many of our members, returning veterans, came together to continue the community spirit that brought Mayfair together while they were away." It was a beautiful autumn day when I met with Bryan at the outdoor ceremony. The event took place on the corner of Lawrence Avenue and Keeler Street in Mayfair, where a permanent memorial had been established to honor neighborhood residents who had distinguished themselves in service to our country. The memorial itself was originally dedicated on November 3, 2001. Instrumental in its conception were Roger McGill and Arthur Bresnahan, two Vietnam veterans who knew the Fitzmaurice family well. The memorial was a labor of love for Roger, Art, and the rest of veterans committee. They knew the tremendous price that their community had paid in going off to fight our nation's wars. These men had known the healing power that was represented in the Vietnam Memorial Wall, and they wanted a small sense of that renewal through remembrance to be present in their own neighborhood that had sacrificed so much.

There were various presentations honoring several veterans from our nation's different conflicts. I stood silently next to Bryan at the back of the crowd, surveying the assembled audience. The honor guards, the numerous dignitaries and politicians, the policemen, firemen, and clergymen all assembled to pay tribute to duty, honor, and country. As I looked out on the attendees, I could not help but think of the immense costs associated with the maintenance of those values. The costs to those we send into harm's way, and those who stand vigil at home, waiting for their loved ones to return.

When it came time to honor Tim Fitzmaurice, his niece, Kristen, and his nephew, Timothy, rose to pay tribute to an uncle they never met. They read excerpts from Tim's combat record, and stories about their uncle from those who once knew him. They spoke impassionedly of an emptiness that they felt for someone who died before they were born. Is it possible to miss someone you never knew? Can you lament the potential that someone may have brought to your life? The words so eloquently expressed by Tim Fitzmaurice's niece and nephew on that day seemed to answer these questions affirmatively.

When the speeches had ended, I told Bryan that I wanted to go up to the front to view the displays that had been laid out for the honorees. As we were walking forward, a woman to my left called the name Bryan. I turned and looked in her direction, and for a moment there was silence. It was Ellen Fitzmaurice Shea. She and Bryan emotionally embraced directly in front of the display stand that honored Tim. Bryan and Ellen were back, with Tim, in the old neighborhood; back where they were young once; back before everything had changed. Many years had passed between them, but for an instance time had not. Tim was together with them now, all these years later. Their youth was gone -- they lost that when Tim was killed -- but they would always have their memories. Memories of being young and the possibilities that youth brings; memories of plans made and plans discarded.

I quickly turned away from them and a wave of emotion came over me. Here was my brother-in-law, Bryan, greeting a woman I had yet to meet, but I already knew of the story, and I could feel the significance of the moment. I would later learn that the Fitzmaurice family considered Bryan as another brother to Tim; and so it was on that autumn afternoon, the surviving family members were together to pay tribute to the sacrifice of their fallen brother.

"And though you may have forgotten all of our rubbish dreams, I find myself searching through the ashes of our ruins. For the days when we smiled, and the hours that we ran wild. With the magic of our eyes, and the silence of our words. And sometimes

I wonder, just for a while, will you ever remember me?"

– Tim Buckley, *"Once I Was"*

The reunion was interrupted as a speaker came to the podium to announce that the ceremonies would continue with a reception held down the street in a church basement. Bryan then turned to me to make the formal introductions to Tim Fitzmaurice's assembled family -- sisters, Ellen and Maureen, brothers-in-law, Dennis and David, and sister-in-law, Maureen. It was decided that we would all head over to the reception where they could talk and catch up on each other's lives. For me it was great to put faces to the names that I had so often heard about. I spent some time getting to know the members of Tim's family. I remember thinking at the time that we so rarely follow the trials of a family who had lost a loved one in war. We are there at the beginning, at the graveside, when the folded flags are handed to the family, and when the caskets are lowered. But for these families, the war never ends and the struggles are ceaseless. Their lives are forever altered. In the case of so many of the Vietnam casualty families, there were the additional feelings that many of us did not share in their grieving. Many of us did not honor their sacrifice. Many of us did not mourn all that these families had lost. Can those families ever forgive us? Should they?

After a few rounds of cake and coffee, it was time to say goodbye. As Bryan said farewell to Tim's sisters, Ellen and Maureen, and the rest of the family, there were tearful plans being made of future get-togethers. Bryan and I then turned and walked up the basement stairs to the street. As we walked back to our cars, Bryan asked me if I wanted to stop for a drink. "I've got something I'd like to show you," he said. We drove a short distance to a tavern just around the corner from the Mayfair Veterans Memorial. I arrived first and took a seat at the bar and ordered a beer. Bryan was not far behind. He sat down next to me, and he placed a large white envelope on the bar. He slid the envelope back behind him while he asked for his drink. We proceeded to talk at length about things that were going on in our mutual family. His three grown children, all with advanced educational degrees, were very busy with their successful lives working in careers that they loved. He spoke proudly and glowingly of his wife of 32 years. Bryan, himself, was in transition. Like many of his generation, he was moving into retirement. His 44 years with Illinois Bell/AT & T -- he started with them one year before he left for Vietnam -- were coming to an end. I asked him if he was nervous about this move into the unknown of life. Bryan told me that he was excited about this new phase. He had plenty of things to do to keep him busy, and was not planning on just sitting around and watching the world pass him by. He talked about

AFTERWORD

heading back to school, and exploring things that there wasn't enough time for while working and raising his family.

It was a common story with so many of the Vietnam veterans whom I had spoken with. Despite their harrowing wartime experiences, and personal tragedies, they came back from Vietnam to take up their lives and form the backbone of our society. Contrary to many of the myths about the Vietnam veteran, 85 percent of them made successful transitions to civilian life after the war. Vietnam veteran personal incomes exceed that of non-veteran age groups by more than 18 percent. 74 percent of Vietnam veterans would serve again, even knowing the outcome. You would think that bitterness would be a pervasive emotion in this generation of veterans. Many of them do, quite justly, hold much contempt for a country which did not welcome their return home from war with gratitude. It seems, at times, that we as a society are trying to play catch-up with respect to our admiration for the Vietnam veteran. Their country called on them to serve and the veterans courageously, and unhesitatingly, answered that call. For many, however, their service was met with vilification and disrespect. Many of our citizens simply could not separate out their feelings about an unpopular war, and those whom we sent to fight it. There have been many healing efforts that have greatly eased some of the pain of these veterans. It simply cannot be overstated how the Vietnam Wall Memorial in Washington, D.C., has served to bind up the psychological wounds felt by this generation of warriors. But for many, a trip to our nation's capital to see this stirring memorial is not possible. There is, however, a Traveling Wall Memorial that moves across the country, giving all Americans a chance to feel the essence of this powerful memorial to the fallen. We have seen the touching images of Vietnam veterans facing

AFTERWORD

The Wall, deep in thought, remembering a friend who never made it home. They stare deeply into The Wall, and it's as if the past is speaking to them. They see in the reflection of the polished granite the person they used to be, or the person that they had hoped to become. We watch the almost sacred ritual of someone taking a pencil rub to an etched name on The Wall in order to leave with an enduring memory of a loved one who stayed behind. The names on The Wall call out to the living, pleading to be remembered.

In the summer of 2011, The Traveling Wall made an appearance at Navy Pier in Chicago. I visited The Wall there and located the name of Timothy G. Fitzmaurice on Panel 57E, Row 20. I immediately saw, by the flowers left at the base of The Wall that a Fitzmaurice family member had been there before my visit. Beside the flowers was a note from Tim's sister, Maureen. "Over 40 years ago our family suffered the loss of my big brother, Timmy. He was truly a remarkable young man and we loved him dearly. I was only 10 years old when he died. I was 8 years old when he went into the Marine Corps. I don't remember a lot about him, but I do know how much I loved him. He was and is my hero. When I was 12 years old, I wrote the following essay for my eighth grade English class. I am sharing this today to let everyone know that he is more than just a name on a wall. He was a beloved son, grandson, brother, nephew, cousin, and friend. His death touched so many people -- including the nieces and nephews that he was never able to meet. May 9, 1968, is the date that changed all of our lives forever."

> *Portrait of A Hero by Maureen Fitzmaurice* -- From the beginning of time there lived many heroes. Their heroic acts are recorded in history books and we become familiar with their names and the wonderful deeds

AFTERWORD

they performed. Some heroes do not get their names in history books, but there are beloved as the ones who are famous throughout the world. There lived a certain young man who can take his place among our nation's heroes. He lived a beautiful life. His boyhood was filled with happy laughter as he served God and his country, first as an altar boy and Boy Scout, and later on as a United States Marine Corporal. He asked to be sent to Vietnam because he felt the country needed our support. Many letters reached our home, written when he was tired and weary after days of fighting the enemy in the bush. He had a job to do and he did it well. As a fire squad leader, he would lead his patrol time after time into the intense jungle. On May 9, 1968, they fought the fiercest battle of all, and then the beautiful, cheerful letters stopped coming. His flag-draped coffin arrived home. A grateful country awarded him with many decorations for his heroic acts, which were received by his grieving family. A flag is raised in front of his home every day. The flag was flown over the Capitol building in his honor and memory. People who pass his home walk a little straighter when they see the gold star shining in the window. They show a little more respect for the flag that waves so proudly. Their patriotism is stronger because of this young man, who lived and died as such a good American. His presence is felt all around. He grew up to be the kind of American who respected his country and his flag, and he was willing to defend both with his courage and strength. He is my hero. He is my brother.

During a lull in our conversation, Bryan Dillon reached to his left, grabbed the large white envelope that he had brought with him, and slid it

AFTERWORD

over to me. Inside the envelope was a hard bound book with a cover photo and title that read simply, "In Loving Memory." The cover photo was of Tim Fitzmaurice in his Marine Corps dress blue uniform. I did not realize it at the time that I opened the envelope, but it would be this Memorial Book which would become the inspiration for my own effort to tell Tim's story, and the impact that his life had on so many others. Inside the front cover was a letter to Bryan from Ellen Fitzmaurice Shea's son, Dennis, explaining the origins of the Memorial Book, and the reasons why it was important to the family that Bryan have one of the only copies.

Dear Mr. Dillon,

Just before Christmas, my Mom and I compiled a Memorial Book for my Uncle Tim. The book contains many documents relating to my uncle's life and death that my

Mom has kept in boxes in our attic. She really didn't feel comfortable keeping such important pieces of our family history buried in our attic, so I helped her create a way to respectfully share the documents with immediate family members for generations to come. Since you and Uncle Tim were practically brothers, it was a given that she wanted you to have a copy. No one else outside our immediate family will receive one. Some of these documents include photos of Uncle Tim in and out of uniform, his official deployment orders, several letters from my Grandmother to Uncle Tim that he never had a chance to read, an official combat summary from actual members of my Uncle's Marine company who were engaged in Operation Houston II alongside Uncle Tim, the telegram that my Grandparents received when they were notified that my Uncle was killed, the official casualty report

AFTERWORD

from the Marines, a collection of letters of condolence from the government, and personal memories of my Uncle written by my Mom, Aunt Maureen, my Dad, and a Marine who was with Uncle Tim when he was killed. We understand that these documents are very emotionally heavy for you, so we understand that you might not flip through the book immediately. However, being that you and my Uncle Tim were practically brothers, it is fitting that you receive a copy."

After reading that poignant and heartfelt letter, I began to page through the start of the book, but Bryan stopped me, and suggested that I take the book home so I could have more dedicated time to absorb the book's contents. But before putting the book back in its envelope, Bryan asked me if it would be all right if he showed me one particular section of the book. He directed me to flip to one of the very last pages in the Memorial Book.

Only later, when I had taken the book home and had time to thoroughly go through it, did I come to grasp the significance of the item which Bryan felt was so important to show me. Bryan had me skip past the pages that displayed the letters of condolences from President Lyndon B. Johnson, Chicago Mayor Richard J. Daley, U.S. Congressman Roman Pucinski, Commanding General of the First Marine Division, Donn Robertson, and Commandant of the Marine Corps, General Leonard Chapman, Jr. We bypassed the pages showing Tim's Purple Heart Citation, the telegram announcing Tim's death, and the copies of the declassified combat reports detailing the hell that the Marines of Mike Company, Third Battalion, Fifth Marine Regiment faced on Hill 1192.

No, all of those pages, all of that information could be looked at later. What was most important for Bryan to show me was buried deep in one of the back pages of the book. There was a page

AFTERWORD

that was a copy of a badly faded checklist form of some sort. At the top of the form in very small lettering was the title "Personal Effects Inventory." The form was a very detailed listing which covered everything from clothes to toiletries. It was exhaustive in its components, and had a description box denoting every conceivable item that a Marine might carry with him into combat. There were additional open lines at the end of the form for any miscellaneous items that were not covered by the preceding list. It was there, at the very bottom of the right hand corner of the list, where Bryan wanted me to look. Typed in, on the final line of the form, was the word "Toy," next to the quantity of "1."

"I wonder what that was," Bryan said to me. It was only later, after I had done the research for the book, after I had heard the stories of what Tim's life had meant to so many others, after I had learned of the indelible mark that

Vietnam had left on all those whose lives were consumed by that conflict, it was only then that I would come back to the powerful significance behind the meaning in Bryan's simple statement of curiosity. Was the toy something that Tim and Bryan had once shared? Was it a toy that Tim had picked up in Vietnam to send back to his young sister? Or was it something that a young Marine carried with him into battle, as a reminder of a place that wasn't filled with death and destruction?

In the haunting book by author Tim O'Brien, *The Things They Carried*, Mr. O'Brien made the case that everything that a "grunt" carried with him into combat had immense significance. When humping the jungles and mountainsides of Vietnam, trying not to get killed; slogging through a miserable existence in oppressive heat and stifling humidity, carrying any extra weight was to be avoided. Hard choices had to be made on what the truly

AFTERWORD

vital things were to have with you in order to make it through alive to the next patrol.

In the introductory vignette of O'Brien's work, the author described each of the book's major characters by detailing what they carried with them into battle -- from physical items such as canteens and grenades and lice, to emotions of fear and love. Tim Fitzmaurice carried Kool-Aid to make the water taste tolerable, and mosquito repellant to keep the bugs away. He carried a Rosary and a Miraculous Medal. He carried letters from his mother and photos of Cindy. And he carried a toy. Because for each life and death struggle that tugged at a Marine every day in Vietnam, there was also knowledge of another world somewhere back home. Tim had parents and grandparents, a brother and sisters, and a girlfriend. There were people who needed him and missed him. Maybe the toy reminded Tim that there was love and caring waiting for him, if he could somehow make it through his war one filthy, exhausting, terrifying patrol at a time. He felt so old in Vietnam, always tired and complaining. The toy told him that he had been young once; drinking beer with friends, playing football, camping in his yard, driving Mom's car, and going to dances with Cindy. They were all young then, their entire generation. Vietnam forced them to grow up in a hurry, making decisions that would reverberate for a lifetime. The time for carrying around toys with them had long since ended. But the recollections of a life before Vietnam were always there. Bryan Dillon's father, Bob, had recalled, with tears in his eyes, a time when Bryan and Tim were playing with toys under the Christmas tree, "I can see Tim over there like it was yesterday." Yesterdays were all that Tim Fitzmaurice had. There were no more tomorrows. They were all left behind on Hill 1192.

I turned once more to look at Bryan, but he was alone now, staring straight ahead, off into the distance of his memories. Then I heard him again, faintly whispering to himself... "Yeah, I wonder what that was".

Me, too.

EPILOGUE

When I was in the beginning stages of the book process, I had a conversation with Ellen Fitzmaurice Shea about the direction that this book would take. I presented her with my point of view of the best way to go about telling the story of the impact of her brother's life. It was my intention from the outset to write the book from an outsider's perspective. I did not want any prospective reader to know my personal connection to some of the main characters in the story until the final chapter. I felt that my relationships should not be a central theme running throughout the book. My goal was to stay focused on Tim's life, and how his untimely death in Vietnam continued to resonate throughout the lives of people today. Ellen, ever patient, waited for me to finish explaining to her my vision on how the book should proceed, and then she went on to put forth a possible angle that I had not considered. She asked me if I had thought about writing the book from the perspective of how I was able to get the main characters to tell their stories. It took me a little while to see from where her idea was coming. Ellen told me that she believed that one of the most intriguing aspects of the writing process could be just my ability to get the stories from those who lived it. From the family members, to the friends, and on to Tim's fellow Marines, many of the story principals were relaying their histories for the first time. They were coming together to remember Tim, but in recalling his impact on their lives, they were reflecting on their own narratives. The book was turning out to be a kind of therapy for those who had repressed some bitter memories over more than forty years. Whatever the feelings were that were coming forth from the people who knew Tim, one thought was universal -- it was time to talk. Maybe they were starting to feel their own mortality. Maybe they wanted their children and grandchildren to know just how those times were for them. Maybe, after more than forty years, it was just too much of a burden to keep the feelings locked up inside. It was time to talk and it was through this book that their voices could be heard. So, had I thought about approaching the book from that angle?

Ellen and I finished our conversation and I promised her that I would give some serious consideration to her thought-provoking suggestion. I was intrigued by her idea, but always had reservations about injecting myself too prominently into the storyline. I wanted the book to focus on, and honor, the courage, sacrifice, and love of Tim Fitzmaurice. This book would belong to him. It was his story that I wanted to tell. Yet, as I moved further and further through the writing exercise, after having sat through one incredibly emotional interview after another, I began to slowly embrace Ellen Shea's vision, and decided that I would incorporate her idea into an epilogue for the book.

It has been one of the great honors of my life to sit down and talk with the inspiring people whose names have graced these pages. Allow me to tell a few stories on how their heroism came to be represented in this book.

Ellen Fitzmaurice Shea and Maureen Fitzmaurice Schiesser -- Obviously, without these two courageous women there would be no book. They put their love for their brother, and the honor that his life story deserved, into the hands of someone whom they had met only

EPILOGUE

once, and someone who had never previously written anything of substance. I had my brother-in-law, Bryan Dillon, contact them with an idea for the book. I followed up Bryan's initial outreach with a phone call to Ellen. I re-introduced myself, and then went on to state my case as to why they should entrust me with telling the tale of their most personal and painful of family memories. Ellen requested a written statement of my vision for the book, and a complete outline detailing my ideas on how the project would be laid out, and where my areas of focus would lie. I provided that to Ellen and then waited on a decision. It was after the decision was in the hands of Ellen and her sister, Maureen, that my first feelings of doubt crept in. I wasn't sure which answer I now wanted to hear. The thought of the family saying "yes" to my book proposal worried me as much as a rejection of the project. A "yes" answer from the family would require me to do the extensive work of research, interview, and writing, in order to turn out a book worthy of the story. The thought of all that effort allowed self-doubt to enter into the picture, and had me wondering if I would be taking on something beyond my capabilities. Conversely, a "no" answer would have left me disappointed, believing that Tim Fitzmaurice's story was truly one worth telling. When the family came back with the decision that they wanted the book written, I was elated. My self-doubt was replaced with a feeling of enormous responsibility. The family was entrusting me with something that was very dear to them. By allowing me to try to give voice to their brother's story, Ellen and Maureen were showing the same courage that had always been a part of who they were. It has been a motivating factor throughout the entire book process -- I hope I haven't let them, or Tim, down.

EPILOGUE

My initial interviews with Tim Fitzmaurice's sisters were solo interviews. As important as their thoughts were together as family, their individual stories on how they came to cope with Tim's death were equally compelling. I was awed as they conveyed to me the impact that Tim's life and death had on their own lives. Each interview was unfailingly emotional, but what caught me off guard were my own reactions to their remembrances. The sadness and despair that they shared with me was intense. Time, definitely, had not healed all wounds. In many instances, time exacerbates old emotions, as people come to grips with the enormity of what their lives have lost when someone they loved has been taken from them too soon. I believed that the sisters may have perceived the book as an opportunity to tell their children and grandchildren of the times that shaped their lives.

Ellen Fitzmaurice Shea, Bryan Dillon, and Maureen Fitzmaurice Schiesser pictured at the Shea family home in the spring of 2013.

I went on to have follow-up contacts with Ellen and Maureen via phone, e-mail, and additional in-person interviews, but it was in those first interviews that I thought that I might have gained their trust. For myself, I felt that I had found new friends, and together we were going

EPILOGUE

to work on a common goal. We were going to pay homage to courage. We were going to remember Tim.

Dennis Shea -- My connection with Ellen's husband, Dennis, was one of the most rewarding relationships that I developed during the project. His wisdom and insight were invaluable to the book. The reason I believe that Dennis' contributions were so important was the fact that he spanned several of the essential themes included in the book. He knew Tim Fitzmaurice personally, he has been a part of the family who has dealt with the reality of a life without Tim, and, lastly, Dennis has lived the horror of Vietnam. These were the interview topics that were on the table for our initial meeting. It would be hard to overstate the intensity that was present during our first talk. Again, you have to realize, I was someone whom Dennis had only recently met, and I was asking him questions of an extremely personal nature. Many of my questions may have been his first attempt to put words to emotions that had built up over 40 years. At times I felt as if I were intruding on the privacy of a fiercely proud and honorable man. Dennis accommodated my inquiries with grace and patience, and for that I owe him a huge debt of gratitude, and my profound thanks.

Bryan Dillon -- It would have been impossible to proceed with a book about Tim Fitzmaurice without the willful and complete cooperation of my brother-in-law, Bryan Dillon. Over the many years that we have known one another, I have had conversations with him about his Vietnam involvement. The talks always left me wanting more information, but I was tempered by the thought that just maybe Bryan didn't care to completely discuss his wartime experiences, especially to someone who wasn't there and who had no real frame of reference to understand what those times were

EPILOGUE

like. The subject of Tim Fitzmaurice was an even more delicate topic. How could I ask Bryan what it was like to lose his best friend? Did I even have that right?

I chose an awkward time to go to Bryan and ask for his cooperation for the book project. We were at a hospital, visiting Bryan's father. Bob Dillon had been courageously dealing with a serious health issue. I chose this time to ask Bryan if I could speak with him briefly in the hospital waiting area. I told him that I had an idea for a book about Tim Fitzmaurice, and if the book ever had a chance of getting off the ground, that I would need his help every step of the way. Despite my insensitivity as to the time and place of asking my brother-in-law about helping me with a book about the life and death of his best friend, Bryan graciously agreed to help. I informed him that I would need him to make the initial inquiries to Tim

Fitzmaurice's sisters, and he told me that he would call them at his first opportunity. It was just the beginning of an idea, but with Bryan's help and guidance, I knew the book project might have a chance.

Bob Dillon -- In preparing to talk to Bryan Dillon's father, and my father in-law, I knew I would be conducting one of my most challenging interviews. He was well into his 80's at the time of the writing of the book, so my goal in broaching such sensitive subject matter was to be delicate and respectful. I wanted to ask him the question that he, and his wife Pat, so surely agonized over after Bryan went to Vietnam. After the cold reality of Tim Fitzmaurice's death in May of 1968, and the horrific casualty reports coming back from Vietnam in the preceding months before Bryan's deployment in November of 1968, the inquiry, I believe, would get to the heart of just what was at stake during those excruciating days

EPILOGUE

of anguish. The interview took place in Bob's living room and I took my time, gingerly getting to the eventual question that I wanted Bob to consider. "Did you think that you might not see Bryan again after he left for Vietnam?" After I asked that of Bob, he hesitated before answering. He then told me, "There was bad news on TV every night back then. We were lucky that Bryan came home alive." Bob stopped talking and put his head down after telling me that. After a moment, he raised his head and said again softly, "We were lucky".

Cindy Moderi -- Cindy was someone whose contribution, I felt, would be essential to the book undertaking. Her openness and her willingness to share some very personal and painful memories allowed me to gain an insight into another side of Tim Fitzmaurice, a side which only she knew. My first contact with Cindy was by phone. I had to leave a message because

Cindy was not available at the time. She told me that when she listened to my phone message, introducing myself and briefly outlining my desire for her input on a book about Tim, she was startled "as if she had seen a ghost." Her memories came instantly flooding back as she re-played my phone message. She returned my call, and after a long phone conversation, told me that she would need some time before deciding how much she would be willing to commit to the book project. When she called back a few days later to let me know that she would do whatever she could to add to the book, I felt that all the pieces were in place to give an accurate accounting of Tim's life story. Cindy and I met at a restaurant for our introductory interview. Her memory for details about Tim, backed by photos and letters, became indispensable to the project. But more importantly, her spirit and her fearlessness have been central to the true essence of the book. I asked Cindy before our

EPILOGUE

initial conversation began if she had any questions for me. "We were just ordinary people, why would you want to write a book about all of us? That simple question from Cindy, posed with humility and grace, formed a guiding foundation for the entire book -- ordinary people who have lived extraordinary lives. While we were leaving the restaurant, after almost two hours of reminiscing about Tim, Cindy told me she felt as if she had known me before. In that moment I felt Tim's presence. He was guiding this endeavor.

Len Swiatly -- In the summer of 2011, The Vietnam Traveling Wall came to Wrigley Field in Chicago in conjunction with an on-field event honoring Chicago's Vietnam veterans, sponsored by the Chicago Cubs baseball organization. Len Swiatly returned to Chicago from his Iowa home to attend the event with myself and Bryan Dillon. Len, Bryan, and Tim Fitzmaurice were high school friends from DePaul Academy.

More than forty years ago they had all gone to war, and as I watched Bryan and Len, each now in his early 60s, standing silently together in front of Tim's name on The Traveling Wall, the true meaning of all they had lost came into focus. Len was wearing the beret from the United States Navy uniform he had worn in Vietnam, and holding a bouquet of flowers that Tim's sister, Ellen Fitzmaurice Shea, had brought to The Wall. He had come home to pay tribute to his friend, Tim. Len came to The Wall to remember someone who had a profound influence on his life. In a way, Tim did make it back from Vietnam, because by carrying Tim's memory lovingly in his heart, Len had allowed their friendship to last a lifetime. They had grown old together because Len had never forgotten Tim. I thank Len for his openness in offering his intensely personal recollections of his lifelong friend.

EPILOGUE

Len Swiatly (L) and Bryan Dillon pictured outside Wrigley Field in Chicago where the Vietnam Traveling Wall made an appearance in 2011. Len holds a bouquet of flowers left at the base of The Wall for his friend, Tim Fitzmaurice.

Jim Quinn -- Jim was introduced to the project through an invaluable contributor to my book research, Roger McGill. Roger had met Jim by chance at a Traveling Wall memorial in Chicago. Both veterans, who had never before met, happened to be searching The Wall, simultaneously, for the same name. Roger, a Saint Edward Parish member, and a Fitzmaurice family friend, was scanning The Wall for Tim's name -- honoring another Saint Ed's kid who had made the ultimate sacrifice. Without knowing it at the time, Roger was standing at The Wall next to the Marine who had put that Saint Ed's kid, Tim Fitzmaurice, in a body bag on Hill 1192. An innocent conversation began between Jim Quinn and Roger McGill, which eventually led both men to realize the emotionally overwhelming coincidence of meeting at the same time and place to pay tribute to Tim. I came to see the story of the fortuitous

EPILOGUE

meeting of these men as another sign in the book journey. I sat with Jim Quinn on two occasions, each gripping interview filled with stirring recollections of his wartime experiences. A Bronze Star and Purple Heart recipient, Jim relayed to me the sheer horror of combat in Vietnam, and the particular devastation that took place on Hill 1192. We were seated in a coffee shop when Jim divulged to me the intense feelings of anxiety and distress that were welling up inside him just sitting and discussing the war with me. His fortitude and his bravery in going back to times and places that he may have wanted to leave unvisited have inspired me greatly.

Roger McGill, Arthur Bresnahan, and Neal Schilling -- I needed the assistance of Roger McGill, once again, to set up a group interview with other Vietnam veterans from Saint

Edward Parish. I was hoping to sit down with some men who knew Tim Fitzmaurice, knew his family, his neighborhood, and knew some of the other Saint Ed's guys who never made it home from the war. I was accompanied to the interview by Bryan Dillon. We sat down with Art Bresnahan, Neal Schilling, and Roger McGill for a "Heroes Breakfast," as I came to call it. My goal was to put my digital voice recorder down in the middle of the table, and hopefully these four men would forget that the recorder was even there. I started with a couple of lead-in questions, and then sat back and listened as these aging warriors started telling each other the stories of the times when they were young.

EPILOGUE

Heroes Breakfast attendees -- Back Row: Bryan Dillon (L) and Roger McGill. Front Row: Neal Schilling (L) and Art Bresnahan

Roger McGill grew up right across the street from Saint Edward Church -- the nuns used to say that he could roll out of bed and be in the middle aisle of church. Roger graduated from DePaul

Academy High School in 1961, and was drafted on June 3, 1964. He served in Vietnam with the United States Army from 1965-1966. His combat unit was the Third Squadron, Fourth Cavalry of the 25th Infantry Division. Roger returned home from Vietnam to work for the phone company, marry, and raise his children. But Vietnam was never far from his thoughts -- specifically, the shameful way that Vietnam veterans had been treated upon their return home from overseas. Roger made it his mission, through his work with the *Vietnam Veterans of America*, to change some of the public perception of the Vietnam veteran. Many in the American public, and astonishingly, even veterans from previous U.S. conflicts, had to be shown that, despite the intense dislike for the war in Vietnam, the warriors themselves were worthy of our admiration and respect. Central to Roger's mission were two significant accomplishments. The first was the 1986 *Chicago Welcome Home Parade*. The parade, in recognition of our

EPILOGUE

Vietnam veterans, was the largest of its kind up until that point. Over 200,000 veterans and their families marched proudly down the streets of downtown Chicago. It turned out to be an incredible and emotional day of healing for these veterans. Roger was the program chairman for that historic event. A second noteworthy accomplishment by Roger was the November 5, 2005, dedication of the Chicago Vietnam Veterans Memorial. Roger was co-Chairman of the undertaking, and instrumental in moving the project forward from conception to completion. Roger has been a tireless advocate for other important causes specific to Vietnam veterans, from a future Illinois State Vietnam Veterans Memorial, to fighting for more recognition of the detrimental effects on our veterans from the exposure to the chemical defoliant, Agent Orange. Throughout all of his inspirational work, Roger has never forgotten the sacrifice and service of his generation of heroes.

Neal Schilling graduated from Saint Edward Grade School in 1960, and DePaul Academy High School in 1964. His mother was great friends with Lubitza Fitzmaurice. Neal began a four-year enlistment with the United States Marine Corps in July of 1964. He was serving with the 1st ANGLICO (Air Naval Gunfire Liaison Company) when he volunteered to go to Vietnam in August of 1966. Serving with South Korean Marines, Neal's ANGLICO unit was responsible for controlling American naval gunfire and close air support in support of South Korean combat operations. He also was part of two-man teams attached to South Korean infantry companies who called in re-supply missions and medevacs from American helicopters and air support from Marine Corps jets. It was on Neal's trip back from his tour in Vietnam that he crossed paths with Tim Fitzmaurice at the Marine Corps Air Base in Cherry Point, North Carolina. It was at Cherry Point where Neal passionately tried to convince

Tim not to volunteer for duty in Vietnam. If only Tim would have listened to Neal's advice and experience. Neal came home from Vietnam to attend school, receiving his bachelor's and master's degrees from Northeastern Illinois University. Neal resides in Saint Edward Parish today, living only two blocks from his boyhood home. He remains a dedicated and committed advocate for issues imperative to Vietnam veterans. Semper Fidelis, Neal.

Arthur Bresnahan graduated from Saint Edward Grade School in 1958, and went on to earn his diploma from Quigley Seminary High School in Chicago in 1962. He enrolled at Loras College and received his bachelor's degree in 1966. Forgoing graduate school, Art instead joined the United States Marine Corps. Art was highly affected by the death of another Marine from Saint Edward Parish by the name of Michael Badsing. Mike Badsing, who was the first Marine from Chicago to be killed in action in Vietnam, had grown up very close to the Bresnahan home. From March 1967 until June 1967, Art was in Officer Candidate School in Quantico, Virginia. He told me that making it through OCS was the hardest thing that he ever had to do. After Quantico, Art went on to the basic school to learn infantry, platoon, and company tactics. His training there was completed in November of 1967, and then it was on to the Naval Air Station in Pensacola, Florida, to learn how to fly various fixed wing and helicopter aircraft. After a final training stop at the Marine Corps Air Station in Santa Ana, California, Art left for duty in the Republic of South Vietnam from September 1969 until October of 1970. During all that training and traveling, Art still had time to marry his wife, Patti, on June 29, 1968. The first of five children was born shortly after Art received his flight wings. A new husband and father, Art shipped out to Vietnam where he flew over 1,000 missions during his tour. When he returned home

EPILOGUE

from the war, he would go on to law school, become a Boy Scout troop leader, a coach, a church choir member, and a father to four more children. Art Bresnahan told me that he saw himself as a "citizen Marine," someone who did his duty for his country, and then came back from his time in the military to build a life of civilian service. "Tim Fitzmaurice should have had that same opportunity. We owe it to all those who never came home to remember everything that they gave up for us." Art still lives in Saint Edward Parish, and many of his children have remained in the neighborhood as well.

I left breakfast that morning after several hours in the company of these incredibly impressive and accomplished men. There was a special bond among all of them. They are proud of their lives, their families, and their service to their parish, their neighborhood, and to their country. They came home from Vietnam and continued to put service above themselves, and improved the lives of others along their life journey.

Frank Pacello, Jim Blankenheim, Dave Burnham, and Jerry Lomax -- Talking with the veterans of the battle for Hill 1192 was especially powerful. There were so many interesting comparisons to be found between those men and Tim Fitzmaurice's family and friends in Chicago. One of the most fascinating components I found when interviewing them was their desire to begin opening up about their experiences. To be sure, the information explosion arising from the Internet was a huge factor in their ability to begin sharing their stories. The capability to connect with other veterans online allowed them to realize that they weren't alone with their thoughts and emotions anymore. By reconnecting with old buddies through the relative emotional safety of email, and group websites devoted to their military units, these men have begun walking through their memories. What they have found is that many of their brothers have carried Vietnam around with them for their entire lives, just as they had. They also learned that war had been over for a long time and a lot of healing had taken place. The mistreatment of the Vietnam veteran had been replaced by an abiding appreciation for all that these men had dealt with in Vietnam, and what they were forced to deal with upon their return. This sentiment was recently played out in the History Channel's documentary *Vietnam in HD*. A veteran by the name of Don Devore spoke of his long-ago instincts to put Vietnam and its effects behind him, but an interesting development had made him want to re-visit those days, "I had taken my Vietnam experience and I had really buried it. I didn't want to bother with it, and I didn't want anyone else to bother me with it. But in my kids' eyes it was a thing of value. That changed my life in a lot of ways at that point. They were very proud of me, very proud of their old man".

But always, these veterans go back to Hill 1192. Over and over in their minds, day after day through their lives, Hill 1192 remains with them. It was important, now, for Frank Pacello and Dave Burnham and Jim Blankenheim and Jerry Lomax to tell us what happened up there. They have never forgotten the faces, and they want us to remember them, too. The faces that fill their minds during the day, and come to haunt them at night. The faces of those who died up there on that hill.

In the days after the battle for Hill 1192, Captain Pacello took the time to write to the families of his fallen Marines. On May 23, 1968, he tried valiantly to console a heartbroken Chicago family with his letter addressed to Lubitza Fitzmaurice. The note read in part:

EPILOGUE

Mrs. Fitzmaurice,

I first want to tell you that while Timothy was with us that he did a fine job as a Marine and we were all really proud of him. I'm very sorry to bother you at a time like this, but I need to tell you that we, too, miss him as a professional Marine and as a very good friend.

Frank Pacello had to write too many of those types of letters during those terrible months of 1968. "I think about those families a lot and what it must have been like to receive such horrible news. I couldn't even imagine how that must have been for them. Talk about them, they're the real heroes," Skipper Pacello implored me.

(On a sad note, Jerry Lomax passed away on August 18, 2012, in Gallatin, Tennessee. A Purple Heart recipient for wounds he received from his gallantry on Hill 1192, Jerry came home from

Vietnam to a career in teaching, followed by over 24 years with the Postal Service. His was the last face seen by Timothy Fitzmaurice before Tim closed his eyes forever. I know I speak for all of Tim's family and friends, when I extend sincere thanks to Jerry for providing some measure of comfort to Tim during his terrifying final moments. Rest in honored peace, Jerry.)

I could go on documenting the many others whose contributions to this project have been considerable; they have my gratitude for their courage and openness in discussing such personal and emotional subject matter. I will end, however, with the most important connection that I tried to make for this book.

If my writing were to have any real meaning, I had to try to connect with Timothy Fitzmaurice. I needed to have a discussion with him -- just the two of us. After talking with all of the incredible

EPILOGUE

people who once knew Tim, I realized that I had to get to know him for myself. I began by paging through the Fitzmaurice family Memorial Book. I would stare at the photos and look into Tim's eyes, trying to gain inspiration on how he would want his story to be told. I visited the family home on Kewanee Avenue, and walked in his yard. I retraced the steps he took in the route from his home to Saint Edward Grade School. I wandered down the hallways of his old school, and I attended services at Saint Edward Church. I looked around his old high school building. I stood outside of the office where he worked, and walked the fields where he played. Lastly, I went to his graveside to talk with Tim, and with God, praying for guidance and inspiration. As I knelt down at Tim Fitzmaurice's gravesite, I finally felt as if we were friends. I was just 45 years too late. I placed my hands on the grass that covered him, and wondered if he was watching me. I asked God to help me find the words to keep Tim alive in the hearts of those who still loved and missed him.

Timothy Fitzmaurice's grave marker in Queen of Heaven Cemetery, Hillside, Illinois. An anonymous floral bouquet is left behind every May 9th.

It was during my attempts to get to know Tim Fitzmaurice that I began to reflect on my own reasons for needing to write this book. What was it about this particular story that inspired me to take my first shot at writing? As far back as I can recall,

EPILOGUE

I had been interested in our country's episode in Vietnam. Obviously, growing up in the late 1960's and early 1970's, I was exposed to the subject of Vietnam through nightly television reports and daily newspaper accounts. I started high school in 1977 and was surprised to discover during those school years that the saga of American involvement in Vietnam was not subject matter that was being covered in the classrooms. If I was going to learn anything of the origins of our intervention in Southeast Asia, and the legacy that the war left behind, it was going to be through self-study. I read as much as I could about the war and its encompassing issues. Beyond the political implications of the conflict, and the incredible courage and professionalism of the American military, my personal interests always returned to the appalling treatment received by those we sent to fight the war upon their return from Vietnam. President Barack Obama remarked in a 2012 Memorial Day speech, while speaking of Vietnam veterans, "You came home and were denigrated when you should have been celebrated. It was a national shame, a disgrace that never should have happened." It was in this context that I wanted to try to tell the story of Tim Fitzmaurice, his family, and his friends. What was it like to sacrifice so much for this country, and be treated so poorly in return?

I also wanted to celebrate Tim, and his family and friends. I wanted to show how all of these people, who suffered so badly, still managed to represent what is best in all of us. Through all of their hardships and disappointments, they never lost their faith, and their hope, that tomorrow would be better than today. They kept the promises that they made to themselves to never forget Tim and to never forget all of the others who shared Tim's dedication and courage. The Vietnam Memorial Wall bears the names of the fallen, but the hearts of those whose names grace the pages of this book bear the grief for the fallen. They have

EPILOGUE

carried that grief for more than 45 years now, and they will carry it until they leave us. They are the best of a generation, and this book is simply a way to say thank you to all of them.

Finally, there was a deeper, more personal reason that I felt gave me the right to believe that I could write about Tim Fitzmaurice. I have no experience with war and its consequences. I have no understanding of that level of service and selfless sacrifice. What I did bring, perhaps naively, to this book endeavor was a sense of destiny. I came to believe in this destiny only after having gone through a traumatic experience in my own life. You see, I, too, once had a brother named Timmy. He was my big brother and my friend. He was funny and supportive, generous and encouraging, and I wanted to be just like him. He shared a date of significance with Timothy Fitzmaurice. Timothy Nicholl was born on May 9, and like Tim Fitzmaurice, there was a light which surrounded him and drew people to him. He inspired my life and I loved him.

Timmy Nicholl committed suicide on December 18, 2007. He was an alcoholic whose life had spun out of his control, so he decided to leave us, without saying goodbye. Like Jack Fitzmaurice, I have struggled with guilt and despair after losing my brother. I will always wonder if I could have done more to help Timmy through his troubles. I owed him so much for all that he meant to my life, yet I wasn't able to see the help that he needed until it was too late.

It has been said that true healing comes to us only when we can think about a lost loved one and those thoughts bring a smile to our face before they bring a tear to our eye. I may not be there yet, but when I witness the stirring example of faith and courage that has been set by the family and friends of Timothy Fitzmaurice, I think I might be able to see the way.

ACKNOWLEDGEMENTS

The guidance and motivation of the following people have been indispensable in the writing of this book:

Timothy Fitzmaurice, Timothy Nicholl, Ellen Fitzmaurice Shea, Maureen Fitzmaurice Schiesser, Dennis Shea, David Schiesser, Bryan Dillon, Susan Dillon, Cindy Moderi, , Len Swiatly, Alex Soraich, Timothy Shea, Michael Shea, Dennis Shea, Bryan Shea, Laurel Schiesser, Kristin Schiesser Paauwe, Kathleen Schiesser, Michael Schiesser, Maureen Dillon, Liam Fitzmaurice, Janice Lee, James and Theresa Nicholl, Robert and Patricia Dillon, Lorraine Swiatly, Danny Boyle, Paul Pennick, Liz Stapleton, Roger McGill, Jim Quinn, Art Bresnahan, Neal Schilling, Jerry Lomax, Frank Pacello, Dave Burnham, Jim Blankenheim, Kelly Harrington Nicholl, James and Susanne Hardy, Mike and Mariann Stanton, Charles O'Donnell and Mike Brennan.

Finally, to my wife, Susan Nicholl, who is an everyday example to me of what it is to live a life inspired - I love you.

Austin J. Nicholl
November, 2013